The Encyclopedia of the
HARLEY-DAVIDSON

The Encyclopedia of the
HARLEY-DAVIDSON

An illustrated directory of the legendary motorcycle marque

MAC McDIARMID

southwater

This edition is published by Southwater

Distributed in the UK by
The Manning Partnership
251–253 London Road East
Batheaston
Bath BA1 7RL
tel. 01225 852 727
fax 01225 852 852

Distributed in Canada by
General Publishing
895 Don Mills Road
400–402 Park Centre
Toronto, Ontario M3C 1W3
tel. 416 445 3333
fax 416 445 5991

Published in the USA by
Anness Publishing Inc.
27 West 20th Street
Suite 504
New York
NY 10011
fax 212 807 6813

Distributed in Australia by
Sandstone Publishing
Unit 1, 360 Norton Street
Leichhardt
New South Wales 2040
tel. 02 9560 7888
fax 02 9560 7488

Southwater is an imprint of Anness Publishing Limited
Hermes House, 88–89 Blackfriars Road, London SE1 8HA
tel. 020 7401 2077; fax 020 7633 9499

© 2001 Anness Publishing Limited

13 5 7 9 10 8 6 4 2

Publisher Joanna Lorenz
Managing Editor Judith Simons
Project Editor Mariano Kälfors
Designer Mike Morey
Jacket Designer DW Design
Production Controller Yolande Denny

Previously published as part of a larger compendium, *The Ultimate Harley-Davidson*

13 5 7 9 10 8 6 4 2

Publisher's note

In recognition of the uniquely American pedigree of the motorcycles featured on the following pages, engine capacity is generally expressed in imperial units (cubic inches) with the metric equivalent (cc) in brackets. However, even Harley-Davidson employ units somewhat arbitrarily, favouring cu in for heavyweight twins, but ccs for Sportster models, a practice we have also adopted.

The capacity of Harley engines should also be treated with some care. Even from the early days, the inch sizes quoted and used by Harley fans were a sort of numeric shorthand, relating only approximately to measured reality. More recently, even the "80-inch" Evo engine actually measured 81.8cu in – a difference of no less than 29cc. In general, where an engine is referred to as something-inch, this refers to popular usage. Dimensions expressed in cu in and/or cc are as accurate as records permit.

We trust that this historical ambiguity will not reduce the reader's enjoyment.

Main front cover image supplied by Mac McDiarmid, all other jacket pictures courtesy of Harley-Davidson Inc.

■ PAGE 1 LEFT *Gordon, Walter Jnr. and Allan Davidson (sitting on bikes), 1929;* CENTRE *William Ottaway, 1924;* RIGHT *Police officers on 1944 UL model*

■ PAGE 3 LEFT *Scott Parker racing on an XR750;* CENTRE *Twin Cam 88 engine;* RIGHT *1999 FLSTF*

■ OPPOSITE *1999 FLHTCUI model*

CONTENTS

INTRODUCTION

What follows is a guide to the major models produced by Harley-Davidson, from the first primitive single of 1903 to the style kings and lavishly-equipped cruisers of today. It is not an attempt to cover every Harley-Davidson model, but all the most important and significant examples are included.

In reviewing machines spanning Harley-Davidson's history, the reader might become aware of one overriding enigma. The company is certainly the most enduring of all the world's motorcycle marques and is currently enjoying an almost unparalleled period of success. Yet, while other motorcycle manufacturers leap headlong into increased technical complexity, Harley-Davidson is as dedicated as ever to its original convictions of sound design and solid simplicity, remaining faithful to its dependable, thoroughbred V-twins.

What Harley-Davidson has in abundance is that indefinable quality called "character" – an attribute no specification panel can reveal. Harley-Davidsons are visceral. They have guts and charisma. Only by riding one can you really begin to understand.

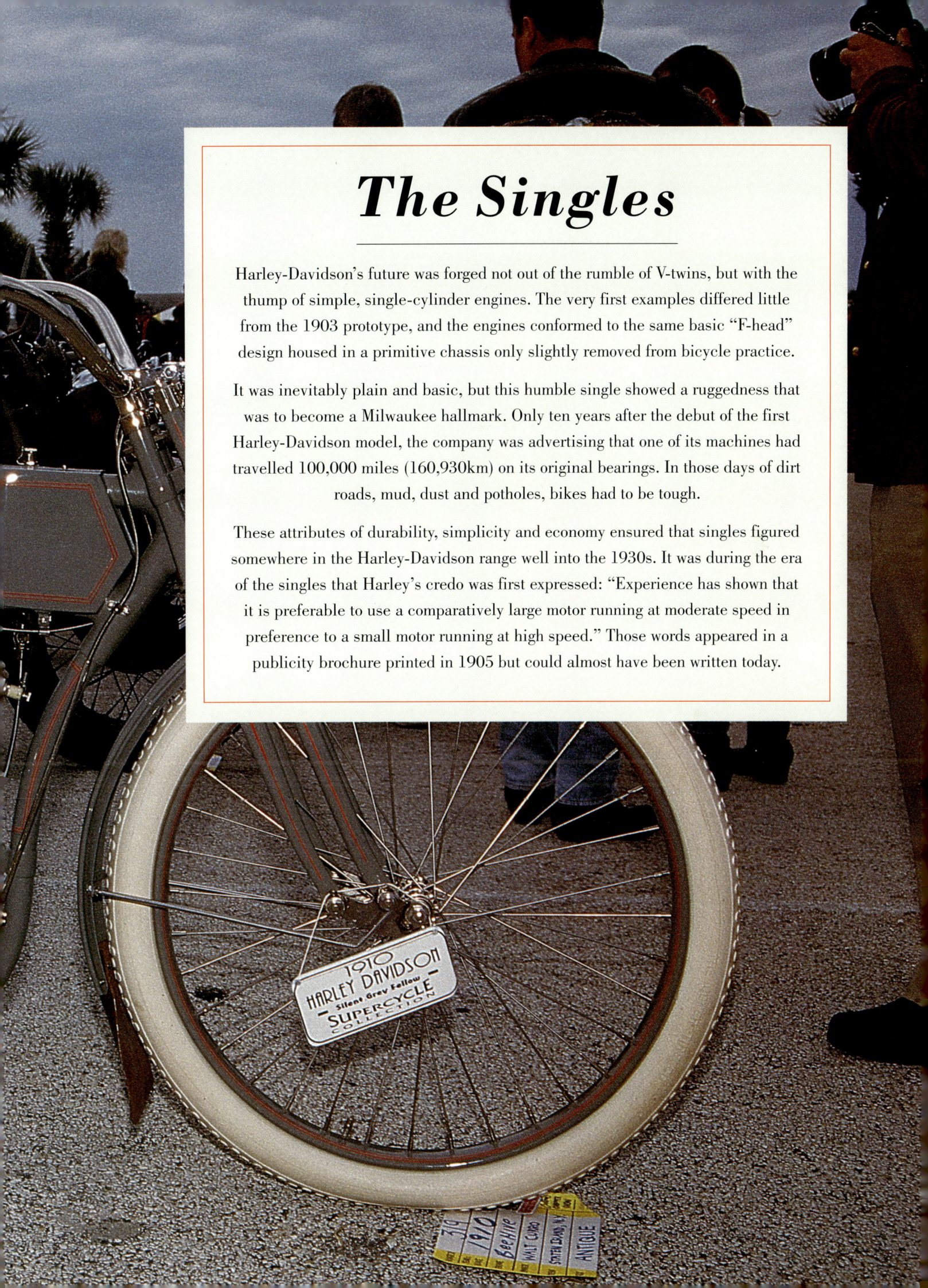

The Singles

Harley-Davidson's future was forged not out of the rumble of V-twins, but with the thump of simple, single-cylinder engines. The very first examples differed little from the 1903 prototype, and the engines conformed to the same basic "F-head" design housed in a primitive chassis only slightly removed from bicycle practice.

It was inevitably plain and basic, but this humble single showed a ruggedness that was to become a Milwaukee hallmark. Only ten years after the debut of the first Harley-Davidson model, the company was advertising that one of its machines had travelled 100,000 miles (160,930km) on its original bearings. In those days of dirt roads, mud, dust and potholes, bikes had to be tough.

These attributes of durability, simplicity and economy ensured that singles figured somewhere in the Harley-Davidson range well into the 1930s. It was during the era of the singles that Harley's credo was first expressed: "Experience has shown that it is preferable to use a comparatively large motor running at moderate speed in preference to a small motor running at high speed." Those words appeared in a publicity brochure printed in 1905 but could almost have been written today.

FIRST SINGLE, 1903–11

■ BELOW AND BOTTOM *One of the first De Dion-Bouton-inspired singles. Pedal assistance was essential on hills. The belt final drive with its crude de-clutching mechanism is clearly seen in the lower photograph. The 1910 "Silent Gray Fellow" is altogether more sophisticated but retains pedals and belt final drive.*

Harley-Davidson's first motorcycle, though nominally a single-cylinder model, evolved with the company over a production span of eight years. During that time, annual production figures soared from fewer than a handful to over 4,000 as demand – and know-how – grew in leaps and bounds. One thing that changed relatively little was the price: $200 in 1904, yet only $25 more by the time production ceased in 1911.

The heart of the engine was a bolted-up crankshaft running car-type, plain, big-end bearings in cast aluminium crankcases. Above this sat a one-piece iron cylinder head and cylinder barrel housing an iron piston. To allow for differential expansion – its top generated far more heat than its bottom – each piston was tapered, a considerable machining achievement for the time. Valve layout was inlet-over-

exhaust, the "automatic" or "vacuum" inlet valve controlled – crudely – via pressure created by the rise and fall of the piston. Removable housing permitted the extrication of both valves for servicing: no method of valve-lash adjustment was available until 1908.

The initial cylinder dimensions of 3 x 3½in (76.2 x 88.9mm) gave a displacement of 24.74cu in (405cc). In 1905, the bore increased to 3⅛in (79.4mm), giving 26.84cu in (440cc). At the same time, the single loop frame was redesigned, as all previous examples

SPECIFICATIONS (1909)	
Engine	single cylinder ioe with automatic inlet valve
Capacity	30.16cu in (495cc)
Transmission	single speed, leather belt drive
Power	around 3.5bhp
Weight	185lb (84kg)
Wheelbase	51in
Top speed	around 45mph (72kph)

showed a tendency to crack at the headstock. Capacity was further increased to 30.16cu in (495cc) in 1909 by a ⅟₁₆in (1.6mm) increase in bore, by which time the exhaust port had also migrated from the side towards the front of the cylinder. Until 1910, all the motors had used horizontal "beehive" finning for both barrel and head; in 1911 this changed to distinctive vertical cylinder head finning.

Lubrication, like almost all engines of the time, was "total-loss" – a gravity feed dripping oil into the engine from a half-gallon (1.9 litre) tank, good for around 750 miles (1,200km). Transmission was of the simplest possible type with a 1¼in-wide (32mm), two-ply leather belt driving the rear wheel directly. There was no gearbox or clutch, although belt tension could be adjusted on the move by 1911.

The starting technique was straightforward, if energetic – run alongside then jump on board and pedal like mad until the motor fired.

A hand-crank starter became available in 1906 for an additional cost, and was standardized the following year, although neither method of starting was notably elegant.

Like modern motorcycles, power was governed by a twist-grip on the right-hand handlebar and a simple "coaster" brake in the rear hub slowed things down. Lighting of any kind was only

made available with the introduction of acetylene lights in the final year of production. Initially, suspension consisted entirely of springs under the leather saddle – and whatever the rider could suffer – but, in 1907, a crude but remarkably effective Sager front fork was added to ease the pain.

As well as standard, conservative "piano" black, by 1906 the single was also available – at an extra cost – in "Renault" pale grey with red pin-striping. This model thus became known from then on as "The Silent Gray Fellow", partly in tribute to its unusually effective silencing. Unpainted metal parts were nickel-plated and the aluminium engine covers were brightly polished to a high shine.

■ ABOVE LEFT *By 1907, the single had grown to 26.84cu in (440cc), was looking more sophisticated and had changed hue: "The Silent Gray Fellow".*

■ ABOVE RIGHT *A 1905 24.74cu in (405cc) single, which cost $200 when new.*

■ ABOVE *A very original 1907 single undergoing restoration work.*

HIDDEN TREASURE

The very first production Harley-Davidson may currently enjoy pride of place behind a bullet-proof glass screen in the Juneau Avenue lobby, but it hasn't always been quite so treasured.

The bike was originally retained by the company and sent to the Pan American Exposition in California in 1915 (since which time Harley has kept at least one example from each year of production). Upon its return, however, the company somehow "forgot" this bike was Number One. During the 1970s, it was damaged in transit to the Rodney C. Gott

Museum in York, but its true identity remained unrealized, even while it was being repaired.

It was only when it underwent a recent comprehensive restoration at the hands of Harley Archives craftsman, Ray Schlee, that the machine's true pedigree was disclosed – by internal parts bearing the legend "Number 1." It is believed to have been raced in 1904 but is now housed in a 1905 frame, as all the earlier examples broke at the headstock.

This unique machine has now been insured for $2 million.

✺ MODEL 5-35 SINGLES, 1913–18

The second-generation single-cylinder machine, produced from 1913 to 1918, housed a refinement of the earlier engine rather than an all-new design. Although the bore remained unchanged at 3⁵⁄₁₆in (84.1mm), the stroke increased from 3½ to 4in (88.9 to 101.6mm), giving a capacity of 34.47cu in (565cc). The new engine was known generically as the 5-35, signifying 5 horsepower and 35 cu in.

Many lessons learned during the troubled development of the first twin were incorporated in the new single's design. Valve layout was still inlet-over-exhaust, although now the inlet valve followed the revised V-twin practice of mechanical operation via a long push rod on the motor's right-hand side. The camshafts – one exhaust, one inlet – were driven by a chain of gears, ending with the Bosch magneto (replaced by a Remy instrument from 1915) which provided the sparks.

■ ABOVE AND BELOW *By the time this Model 9-B was built in 1913, chain drive was a factory option on single-cylinder machines and twins. Both the chain-drive and belt-drive singles cost the same: $290, $60 less than the twin.*

As before, the iron cylinder head and barrel were one-piece, accommodating a steel three-ring piston. The crankcases were of aluminium, in which a high-grade steel crankshaft ran on phosphor-bronze main bearings, with the whole crank assembly balanced. Lubrication was still total-loss, engine oil being metered by hand from its own compartment in the tank slung beneath the frame's top rail. A sight-glass below the tank gave the rider some idea how frequently to deliver drops of oil. As well as manipulating this, the rider was required to adjust the degree of ignition advance (in other words, the precise point at which the spark plug ignited the mixture), by means of yet another control lever. In those days, getting the best out of an engine was not a simple business. It demanded considerable awareness from the operator.

Perhaps the most obvious difference between these early singles was the replacement of belt with chain as the drive medium, eliminating the wet-weather slip that plagued all leather belt drives. On early examples, the drive was taken direct, via roller chain, from a sprocket on the left-hand end of the crankshaft to another on the rear hub. The same hub also contained a type of rudimentary clutch operated by a long lever on the left side of the machine. Starting involved placing the machine on its stand, which lifted the rear wheel off the ground, then vigorously rotating the bicycle-type pedals. These same

SPECIFICATIONS	
Engine	ioe single
Capacity	34.47cu in (565cc)
Transmission	1-, 2- and 3-speed
Wheelbase	55in (1,400mm)
Top speed	around 54mph (87kph) (side-valve) or 65mph (105kph) (ohv)

■ BELOW *All three images show a two-speed Model 10-C from 1914. The single-speed Model 10-B proved far more popular.*

■ BOTTOM LEFT *Harley's astonishingly complex two-speed rear hub is clearly visible in this view. The hub employed a ring of interlocking bevel gears to vary the final drive ratio.*

pedals, when rotated backwards, engaged the "coaster-type" rear brake via a chain on the right-hand side. Lever-operated brakes did not appear until 1918.

A "step starter" and Harley's first two-speed rear hub arrived in 1914 (also in the V-twin), offering increased flexibility with maximum speeds of around 54 and 65mph (87 and 105kph) in the two ratios. Within a year, this deceptively intricate device had given way to three-speed transmission with a true sliding-pinion gearbox on better-specified models. Nonetheless, single-speed and even belt-drive models continued to be built for some years.

Chassis refinements included a more robust front suspension offering around 2in (50mm) of travel. The rear, of course, would remain rigid for many years. However, a degree of consolation was provided by Harley's patented "Full Floteing" seat.

As well as the paired springs common on other motorcycles, this seat featured a hinge at the front and a coil spring inside the seat post to cushion the rider from the worst of the bumps.

■ BELOW *Although it retained pedals, the two-speeder offered footboards for the first time. Note the ignition magneto which is below the carburettor.*

MODELS A & B SINGLE, 1926–34

Although single-cylinder machines were as much a hallmark of Harley-Davidson's formative years as the big V-twins with which they are now associated, Juneau Avenue produced almost no such models from 1919 until 1926. The sole exception was the Model CD, a 37.1cu in (608cc) machine created by the simple expedient of removing one pot from the 74-inch twin. It was built in very small numbers from 1921 to 1922 and was intended for commercial use only. When singles did reappear, they were considerably smaller than before, displacing just 21.1cu in (346cc) compared to the earlier 30-inchers.

Somewhat confusingly, the single was known simultaneously as both Model A and Model B. The former denoted a magneto version, the latter that the

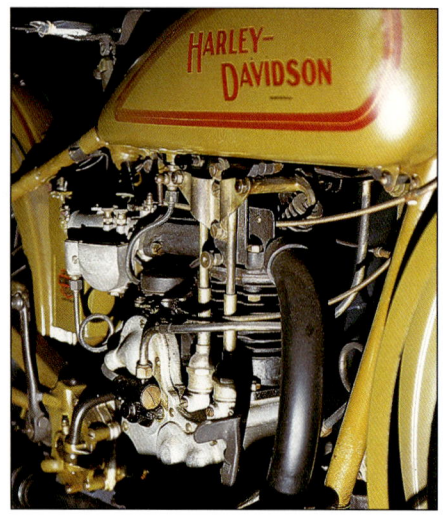

machine was fitted with a generator and coil ignition. This was further refined into Models AA and BA Sport Solos, where the second letter indicated that the engine had overhead valves. The

■ ABOVE *The ohv "Peashooter" engine. The push-rods, rocker arms and exposed valves are clearly visible.*

■ LEFT *Dual "bullet" headlights first appeared on this 1929 500cc single, derived from the Models A and B. Note the front brake – another novelty introduced the previous year.*

SPECIFICATIONS	
Engine	side-valve or overhead valve single
Capacity	21.1cu in (346cc)
Transmission	3-speed
Power	8bhp (side-valve) or 12bhp (ohv)
Wheelbase	55in (1,400mm)
Top speed	around 50mph (80kph) (side-valve) or 60mph (96kph) (ohv)

more basic model, designated by a simple A or B was of straightforward "flathead" design, with valves side-by-side and operated by short push-rods.

The overhead-valve model was an altogether more potent piece of machinery that would achieve considerable competition success as the legendary Peashooter racer. It was inevitably less aggressive in roadster trim, yet still capable of what was then a giddy 4,800rpm and close to 65mph (105kph). Its side-valve sibling, on the other hand, struggled to exceed 50mph (80kph). Despite this marked difference, both engines were rated at 3.31 horsepower. At the time, quoted power figures were not a measure of actual output, merely a function of piston displacement and thus quite meaningless as a reflection of performance. Modern power figures, of course, describe actual output. Strangely, Harley chose to promote the flathead at the expense of the more advanced engine, probably because side-valves would soon comprise the vast bulk of the Milwaukee range.

Mechanically, the engine featured a lightweight aluminium alloy piston

■ LEFT *Stripped-down racing version of the ohv "Peashooter". Note low, pulled-back handlebars and spartan saddle.*

(initially iron for the side-valve machines) running in a cast-iron cylinder. Typically for the time, the overhead's valve gear was exposed, although the 21.1 cu in (344cc) single was the first Milwaukee engine lubricated by a proper mechanical pump. Nonetheless, a hand pump was retained for supplementary oiling when the engine was under extreme loads. Transmission was by the now-familiar three-speed sliding gear, driven by a foot-operated single-plate dry clutch.

By the time of the new single's debut in 1926, electrical equipment had leaped forward in specification and dependability. Although full electrical equipment was optional (Models A and AA came as standard with just a magneto to generate sparks), it was also comprehensive. Generator models featured a coil and distributor (to power and time the ignition), battery, horn, two-bulb headlight and tail-light, all controlled from a switch on the steering

head – everything you might expect to find on a modern motorcycle, except stop-light and indicators. Less can be said for the cycle parts. True, the single wore the new type of teardrop petrol (gas) tank, which wrapped over the top frame tube rather than hung from it, as

before. At the front, Harley's familiar sprung forks gave some comfort and control, but the rear end was rigid and would remain so for more than 20 further years. The rear hub did contain a brake – a 5¾in (146mm) drum – but the front wheel contributed nothing to retardation. It would be another two years before Milwaukee installed their first front brake. During the early 1930s, "21"'s sales were hit, partly by the relative success of the Series C single, but mainly by the Depression. Domestic supplies were halted during 1931 when just three examples were exported. The ohv model never reappeared, although flathead sales rallied slightly before the model was axed at the end of 1934.

■ ABOVE RIGHT *Note the gear lever (left) and fillers for oil and fuel. The switch console is a later addition.*

■ RIGHT *Although only $40 cheaper, flatheads such as this Model 26-B solo comfortably outsold the more exotic ohv singles.*

MODEL C SINGLE, 1929–34

In 1929, the Model A and B singles got a bigger brother with the introduction of the Model C. Displacing 30.1cu in (493cc), the newcomer's top end was essentially half of the old 61-inch Model F/J twin, mated to the 21-inch single's bottom end. This was clearly a more sound solution than the trick many American racers had been pulling for years – they had simply removed one top end and connecting rod from the J, blanked off the hole and let rip on the track. Road riders demanded something slightly more elegant.

Unlike the "21" however, this time no overhead-valve variant was offered; the model was resolutely side-valve, although the greater pulling power of the 30-inch motor meant that, for the modest uses for which most singles were destined, no overhead valves were required. Power was sufficient for a top speed approaching 60mph (96kph).

Compared to the smaller single, the "30" was both bored and stroked with even more undersquare dimensions of 3¹⁄₁₆ x 4in (78.6 x 101.6mm). Since it

SPECIFICATIONS

Engine	side-valve single
Capacity	30.1cu in (493cc)
Transmission	3-speed
Power	10bhp
Wheelbase	57½in (1,460mm)
Top speed	around 56mph (90kph)

was also slower revving than the "21", a 42 per cent increase in capacity realised only a 25 per cent increase in power, from eight to ten horsepower. Both machines shared a similar three-speed transmission. An overhead-valve competition derivative, the Model CA (later CAC) was produced in very limited numbers. By the time of the Model C's debut in 1929, Harleys had begun to develop front brakes (they also

■ ABOVE *This Series C 500cc 3-speed single shows the low-line frame introduced in 1930.*

■ LEFT *A 1929 500cc single. At the time, the vibrant paint job was optional only on twins.*

featured on the 45-inch twin that appeared in the same year). Like the rear brake, this was a simple, single-leading shoe drum, but activated by a lever on the right handlebar, as is the practice today.

Early examples shared the same frame and running gear as contemporary 21-inch singles, but during the second year of production the larger engine was installed in a chassis "borrowed" from the twin. This turned the robust little single into a "full-size" motorcycle – ironically with a lower seat height but increased ground clearance.

More ironically still, in 1933 it was joined by the Model CB, essentially a 30-inch engine in 21-inch running gear

– a choice perhaps prompted by excess stock of the latter.

Worthy as the Model C was, the majority of American motorcycle buyers still hankered after twin-cylinder pulling power even during the depths of the Depression.

A measure of the singles' problem at home was that, during 1929, sales of the 21- and 30-inch singles combined were little more than half of those of the Series D twin – 3,789 units compared to 6,856.

Nonetheless, though comparatively unheralded in their own country, the sturdy little singles proved popular overseas as Harley-Davidson continued to develop its international markets,

■ **ABOVE** *This mammoth modern ElectraGlide might look a far cry from the early singles, but they are very much its ancestors.*

where the sheer weight and size of the big twins often posed problems to potential buyers. Not surprisingly, the larger single had soon became the dominant seller.

Initially priced at just $20 more than the $235 price-tag of the "21", the Model C comfortably outsold the smaller machine from 1930 onwards. More than 5,000 units of the popular Series C were produced in total over the life span of the model, which was to be six years in all.

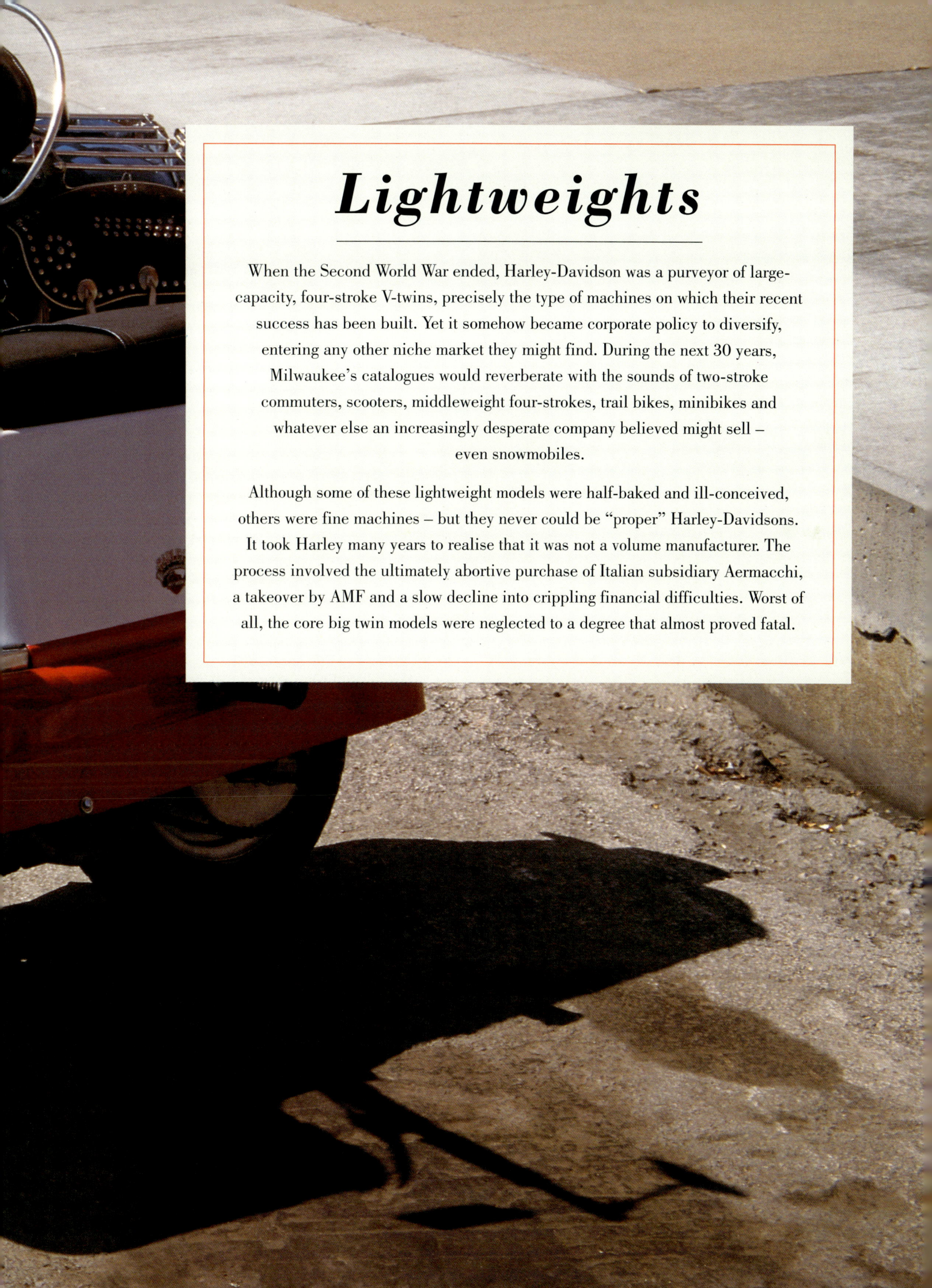

Lightweights

When the Second World War ended, Harley-Davidson was a purveyor of large-capacity, four-stroke V-twins, precisely the type of machines on which their recent success has been built. Yet it somehow became corporate policy to diversify, entering any other niche market they might find. During the next 30 years, Milwaukee's catalogues would reverberate with the sounds of two-stroke commuters, scooters, middleweight four-strokes, trail bikes, minibikes and whatever else an increasingly desperate company believed might sell – even snowmobiles.

Although some of these lightweight models were half-baked and ill-conceived, others were fine machines – but they never could be "proper" Harley-Davidsons. It took Harley many years to realise that it was not a volume manufacturer. The process involved the ultimately abortive purchase of Italian subsidiary Aermacchi, a takeover by AMF and a slow decline into crippling financial difficulties. Worst of all, the core big twin models were neglected to a degree that almost proved fatal.

STATESIDE STROKERS

■ MODEL S-125, 1948–52
MODEL ST-165, 1953–9
MODEL B HUMMER, 1955–9

Harley-Davidson's first venture into the world of two-strokes owed much to the end of the Second World War. On the one hand, it was assumed that thousands of demobbed GIs would crave almost any motorcycle they could lay their hands on, and the 125cc single was considered the ideal low-cost candidate. Second, the design was basically that of the pre-war DKW RT125.

When partition placed the factory in the new East Germany, the design passed to the Allies as war reparations. British BSA's hugely successful Bantam was also a DKW copy, as was the very first Yamaha, the YA1 "Red Dragonfly".

Producing just three horsepower from its simple piston-ported, air-cooled engine, the S-125 must have been a profound disappointment to any American biker raised on big four-stroke power.

Juneau Avenue was evidently hopeful about selling these machines in huge

SPECIFICATIONS: S-125	
Engine	2-stroke single-cylinder
Capacity	125cc
Transmission	3-speed
Power	3bhp
Wheelbase	50in (1,270mm)
Top speed	around 40mph (64kph)

numbers, producing more than 10,000 in the model's first year, but sales proved poor, settling to around 4,000 per annum even after the introduction of a "Tele-Glide" version with telescopic forks in 1951.

A bore increase in 1953, from 52 to 60mm, resulted in the slightly zippier 165cc Model ST. A restricted version, the STU, was also available.

Two years later, the Model B Hummer – using essentially the same 125cc engine and transmission as the first Model S – appeared in the Harley-Davidson catalogue.

From 1960 to 1961, an updated 165cc range continued as the 6bhp BT and BTU (restricted to 5bhp) Super Ten. Harley-Davidson's slogan for this model went: "keen wheeling for teen wheeling".

■ ABOVE *The ST-165: the striking quartered tank emblem dates from 1957.*

■ LEFT *The first two-stroke was this Model S of 1948. Note the girder front forks.*

■ **BELOW** *The Pacer was the pure street version of the Model BT range of 165 and 175cc two-strokes.*

■ **BOTTOM** *A Topper in conventional livery. Although quite advanced, the $450 machine failed to cash in on the scooter boom.*

■ **BELOW** *A Topper Scooter, now used as Harley's corporate paddock transport.*

■ RANGER, PACER, SCAT, BOBCAT, 1962–6

This quartet was another attempt to broaden the Harley range and allow Milwaukee to compete as a mass-market player. In hindsight, the strategy was clearly misguided, but Milwaukee believed there was a niche market of buyers not quite ready for the new 250cc Sprint (nor for the big twins). The Ranger and its siblings were the result.

All four machines, designated Model BT, shared a two-stroke engine derived from the Super 10, but with increased stroke from 60 to 61mm for a capacity of 175cc on all but the 1962 Pacer and Ranger. As with the Topper, "full power" and 5bhp versions were built.

Models that year were the street-only BT Pacer, the dual-purpose BTH Scat and the BTF Ranger, a stripped-down, off-road variant without lights. The first examples had rigid rear ends, but

models that had swinging-fork suspension appeared for 1963.

The Ranger was dropped for 1963 while the Pacer and Scat gave way to the BTH Bobcat in 1966.

Available in road and optional off-guises, this lasted for one year, proving to be the last of the American-built Harley lightweights.

■ TOPPER SCOOTER, 1960–5

The Model A Topper – which was Milwaukee's obvious attempt to cash in on the scooter boom which swept the Western world during the late 1950s – employed a 165cc two-stroke with identical bore and stroke to the old ST but with the cylinder laid down horizontally to reduce engine height.

Power was claimed to be 9bhp from the 1961-on high-compression engine (Model AH), with a "restricted" five-horsepower version (Model AU) sold in those American states which permitted the use of low output two-wheelers without a driver's licence.

Unlike earlier three-speed Harley strokers, this time the "Scootaway" transmission was automatic, using belt drive and variable flanged wheels to change ratios.

The system was unusual but by no means new – the Rudge Multi and

SPECIFICATIONS: TOPPER	
Engine	2-stroke single-cylinder
Capacity	165cc
Transmission	variable belt
Power	5bhp or 9bhp
Wheelbase	51.5in (1,310mm)
Top speed	around 50mph (80kph)

American-built NeraCar had featured similar drives decades before – yet it did anticipate today's fully automatic commuter machines.

Other Topper novelties included a rubber-mounted engine with reed-valve induction, a parking brake, under-seat stowage space and lawnmower-style hand-starting.

By all accounts, the boxy Topper was a quirky but competent device which might have fared better had it not arrived just as the scooter market went into decline.

Sales of the $430 machine went from almost 4,000 to just 500 during its six years on the books.

Ironically – given that Harley-Davidson by then had an Italian factory – being "Made in Milwaukee" was no substitute for the true Latin style of other more genuinely Italian scooters, such as those that were made by Vespa or Lambretta.

SPECIFICATIONS: BOBCAT	
Engine	2-stroke single-cylinder
Capacity	175cc
Transmission	3-speed
Power	8bhp
Wheelbase	52in (1,320mm)
Top speed	around 60mph (96kph)

FORZA HARLEY

■ SPRINT, 1961–74

The Sprint family of four-stroke singles, unveiled in September 1960, was the first tangible result of Harley-Davidson's purchase of the Aermacchi concern in Varese, Italy. Compared to much contemporary Milwaukee hardware, this was a technically advanced machine derived from the existing 250cc Ala Verde model, with an in-unit overhead-valve engine and superb handling from its spine frame, telescopic forks and swinging-fork rear end. With its unmistakable horizontal cylinder, variants of the same engine went on to innumerable race wins, including the famous Isle of Man TT, and remain hugely popular (and competitive) in classic racing today.

American buyers – despite the invitation to "thrill to the dynamic, virile note of its Hi-Flo tuned exhaust" – never quite warmed to the Sprint's lack of cubes and relatively revvy nature, yet the bike was as capable a standard production machine as its siblings were racers. The stock street version, the

■ BELOW *Note the carburettor's steep downdraught angle, which is a hallmark of Aermacchi design.*

SPECIFICATIONS: SPRINT C (SS-350)

Engine	ohv horizontal single
Capacity	246cc (344cc)
Transmission	4-speed (5-speed)
Power	18bhp @ 7,500rpm (27bhp @ 7,000rpm)
Weight	unknown (355lb/161kg)
Wheelbase	52in/1,320mm (56in/1,420mm)
Top speed	around 75mph/120kph (85mph/136kph)

Model C, claimed a potent (if slightly ambitious) 18bhp at 7,500rpm from its eager, free-breathing engine. This was joined by the Model H, an off-road variant, one year later, with high-compression pistons and an additional 1.5bhp. The "H" quickly became the more popular model and was used in a wide range of American competitions, from flat track to motocross as well as for purely recreational use.

The Sprint Model H later became known as the Scrambler, producing as much as 25bhp at a relatively giddy 8,700rpm.

In 1967, the original long-stroke configuration changed to short stroke – "The Sprint holds two land speed world records, so we improved it", went the ad. Two years later, the first 350 Sprints appeared, the ERS dirt racer and road-going 350cc SS. The SS was joined by the dual-purpose SX-350 in 1971 and given an electric starter two years later as the "Sprint" title was dropped from the range.

Pure road racing examples of the same 344cc single produced as much as 38bhp, good for 130mph (210kph) with

■ BELOW *This early Sprint enjoys pride of place in the Harley Museum.*

racing streamlining. Road riders, with maybe 25bhp, had to be content with top speeds in the low nineties. Although a simple spine frame was always good enough for the racers, the final SS-350 inexplicably included a heavy and wholly unnecessary twin-downtube chassis.

With a career spanning 14 years, the Sprint can rightly be regarded as one of Harley's more successful forays away from its core big twin-activities.

The Sprint's arrival coincided with the appearance of advanced, lightweight machines from Japan and, to some extent, it profited from their success.

For the first time since the 1920s, motorcycling in the United States was developing a broad appeal, and the market was soaring.

In 1971 it would peak at 2.1 million new machines sold – a 40-fold increase in less than 20 years.

The Sprint's weakness was not the way it went (when the typically feeble Italian electrical system was not playing up), but in the way its price kept rising when Japanese machines seemed, year after year, to be offering much more for much less.

SPECIFICATIONS: M-50	
Engine	2-stroke single-cylinder
Capacity	50cc
Transmission	3-speed
Wheelbase	44in (1,120mm)
Top speed	around 40mph (64kph)

■ BELOW *Trying hard to look like a "real" bike, this 1967 M-50 sports saddlebags and screen, despite a top speed of only around 40mph (64kph).*

■ **M-50, M-65, 1965–71**
In the mid 1960s Harley-Davidson's quest for wider markets led it into the 50cc domain, a move which was ultimately no more successful than its other oddballs of the time. Ironically those other V-twin warlords, the British Vincent company, had dabbled unsuccessfully with lightweights a decade earlier.

The range began with the M-50 in 1965 and a racer-looking Sport version 12 months later. Both were built in huge numbers – more than 25,000 in the first two years – causing massive oversupply and a sharp fall in price. 1967 brought an increase in capacity for the M-65 and Sport, and more realistic production figures.

For 1967, the original 50cc version developed much-needed extra power with the 65cc M-65, by which time some 4,000 unsold M-50s were flooding the market at knock-down prices.

Both models were available in standard and "Sport" guise, the latter with a racy fuel tank and seat.

A 65cc Leggero (which in Italian means "light") version was also built for the years 1970–1.

STRIVING FOR SALES

■ RAPIDO, TX, SX, STX, 1968–77

The Rapido family of machines was yet another attempt to find a profitable niche at the lightweight end of the market, this time with mainly off-road machines (although the first batch to be built were street bikes). Powered by a simple 123cc two-stroke single with four-speed transmission, the Rapido ultimately gave way to the five-speed, oil-injected TX, SS and SX models. Although often overlooked – not least by traditional big-twin dealers – the range established its pedigree in 1969 when three Rapidos completed an epic, 2,000-mile (3,200km) ride across the Sahara, from Morocco to Nigeria. A smaller version of the TX, the 90cc Z-90, was produced.

■ SS AND SX SERIES, 1974–8

By the start of the 1970s, off-road machines were huge business in the American motorcycle scene. Inevitably, this market was hugely competitive, with prices pared to the bone – so much so that even the super-efficient Japanese factories would soon find themselves with massive amounts of unsold stock.

SPECIFICATIONS: RAPIDO	
Engine	2-stroke single-cylinder
Capacity	123cc
Transmission	4-speed
Wheelbase	48.9in (1,240mm)
Top speed	around 60mph (96kph)

At the same time, environmental concerns were targeting the high hydrocarbon emissions of the two-stroke engine. It was into this unpromising scene that the off-road SX range was launched for 1974. The SX was joined by the street-only SS-250 in 1975 plus its larger dirt sibling, the SX-250, with

the road-going SS-175 introduced for 1976. It was the off-roaders, however, that dominated production and sales. More than 25,000 machines were built in 1975, of which all but 3,000 were SX models. In the face of declining demand and over-supply, production slumped to 12,000 for 1976, then 1,400 in 1977 before disappearing almost completely as Harley-Davidson disentangled itself from its Italian partner in 1978.

These were actually quite competent motorcycles despite being very much copies of Yamaha's DT-series engines. The SX-250 in particular achieved quite striking competition success. More successful still was the MX250, derived from what was substantially the same engine. Both failed to survive the closure of Harley-Davidson's Italian operation in 1978.

■ **TOP** *Models such as this 1970 Rapido attempted to cash in on the Stateside boom in lightweight off-road machines.*

■ **LEFT** *An SX-250, one of the Italian two-stroke singles which tried to cash in on the trail-bike boom.*

SPECIFICATIONS: SX-175 (SX-250)	
Engine	2-stroke single-cylinder
Capacity	174cc (243cc)
Transmission	5-speed
Wheelbase	56in (1,420mm)
Top speed	around 70mph/112kph (80mph/128kph)

■ RIGHT *Outlandishly racy, maybe, but such dual-purpose lightweights were too far from Harley's heritage to succeed.*

SPECIFICATIONS: BAJA SR-100	
Engine	2-stroke single-cylinder
Capacity	98cc
Transmission	5-speed
Wheelbase	52in (1,320mm)
Top speed	around 60mph (96kph)

■ **BAJA, SR-100, 1970–4**
Named after the notorious desert race down Mexico's Baja peninsula, this 98cc off-roader used a high-performance engine derived from the Rapido's (with the bore reduced from 56 to 50mm) but now with five-speed transmission. The little machine was surprisingly potent and almost 7,500 were built during its five year span. It was ultimately unable to overcome both environmental concerns and the increasingly sophisticated Japanese competition, despite the introduction of an improved, oil-injected SR-100 version for 1973.

■ **MINIBIKES: SHORTSTER, X-90, Z-90, 1972–5**
Anything further removed from big-inch cruisers would be hard to imagine, but that's exactly what Harley unveiled with the MC-65 Shortster of 1972. An obvious word play on "Sportster", the minibike used the M-65 engine and tiny 10in (254mm) wheels. Only 800 Shortsters were made before it grew to 90cc and became the X-90, which was built from 1973 to 1975. The Z-90 used the same engine, but in a quasi off-road chassis with larger wheels. "The Great American Freedom Machine" was how Harley billed the Italian-built two-

SPECIFICATIONS: X-90	
Engine	2-stroke single-cylinder
Capacity	90cc
Transmission	4-speed
Wheelbase	40.75in (1,035mm)
Top speed	around 55mph (88kph)

strokes, intended mainly for hitching on the back of a camper van rather than as serious commuter machines. Almost 17,000 of these minibikes were made, plus a similar number of Z-90s.

■ **SNOWMOBILE, 1970–5**
Like the Topper Scooter, Harley's Snowmobile was a tardy response to a passing craze. The fad initiated by the Canadian Bombardier company in the mid-1960s produced many similar machines, most with the same mechanical layout. Milwaukee's version, released in 1970, was steered by paired skis linked to motorcycle-type handle-bars at the front and driven by a broad belt at the rear. It was powered by a twin-cylinder two-stroke engine and the all-chain drive featured automatic transmission. There were two capacities (398 or 433cc) and electric or manual start. The Snowmobile was dropped from 1975, the victim of three consecutive mild winters.

■ LEFT *The X-90. Dismissed as "a menace" at the time, the minibike range is now considered cute and even collectible.*

■ RIGHT *Harley's snowmobile sold poorly. Maybe if they'd called it a SnowGlide…*

The First Twins

From a modern perspective, the expressions "Harley-Davidson" and "V-twin" are practically synonymous, yet it was not always so. Expanding the Harley range from singles to twins was a logical progression as Harley attempted to broaden its share in the rapidly expanding American market. The first American V-twin was the 695cc Curtiss of 1903 and Harley's first prototype was built three years later, making its first public appearance at the Chicago motorcycle show in 1907.

Exactly two years later, the Model 5-D twin was offered for sale, with the 45-degree configuration that is now a Harley hallmark. In almost every other respect, however, the engine was entirely different. As with the contemporary singles on which it was based, the F-head valve layout was inlet-over-exhaust, with the inlets of the "automatic" type, in which the valve was simply "sucked" open by the falling piston rather than being moved mechanically by a cam. After almost two decades of painstaking evolution, the F-head layout culminated in the legendary JH and JDH twin-cam models, the "superbike" race replica machines of their day.

As the 1920s drew to a close, side-valve engines became the Milwaukee norm, heralding an era dominated by flatheads such as the enduring "45" and the mammoth 80-inch VL – machines that put the muscle into Milwaukee.

EARLY TWINS

With the single having amply demonstrated its ruggedness, the twin that evolved from it ought to have been the same – only more so. Like the singles, the twin was single-speed with belt final drive, one-piece heads and barrels with horizontal "beehive" finning. Capacity was 53.7cu in (880cc), although several development engines of varying capacity had been built and even raced during the previous two years.

Yet the Model D proved remarkably troublesome, with a mere 29 built in 1909 and just one in 1910. Harley-Davidson appears to have blamed its shortcomings on its automatic inlet valves, although other sources suggest slippage of the belt drive was at fault. Either way, when the re-engineered twin returned in 1911, it had both mechanical inlet valves and a simple but sturdy belt tensioning device which could be operated on the move by the rider's left hand.

Although still designated the Model D, other changes included a slightly reduced capacity of 49.5cu in (811cc), from a bore and stroke of 76.2 and 88.9mm respectively, the same as the

SPECIFICATIONS: 1911 MODEL D	
Engine	F-head V-twin
Capacity	49.48cu in (811cc)
Transmission	single speed, leather belt drive with freewheel "clutch"
Power	around 7bhp
Wheelbase	56½in (1,435mm)
Top speed	around 60mph (96kph)

■ ABOVE RIGHT AND BELOW *Two views of another 1913 twin. Note the long push-rods to the inlet valves, far more dependable than the earlier "automatic" mechanism. The colour is "Renault Gray".*

1904 single. Beehive finning had also given way to vertical cylinder-head finning. At $250, the asking price was the same as the twin of 1908.

By all accounts, the revised twin proved far more dependable than its troublesome predecessor. Although little faster on the flat than the 30-inch single, it climbed hills far better – not least because the belt tensioner allowed the rider to maintain drive. Even so, a welter of improvements followed year on year. 1912 brought a new frame and a free-wheel clutch assembly in the rear wheel that freed the rider from the need to kill (and re-start) the engine if wishing to halt the machine. The same year saw the introduction of the first "one-litre" Harley, the 61-inch X8E, which also featured chain final drive. Although the two capacities were briefly produced in tandem, production of the smaller twin was dropped for 1913. The same year marked the debut of the

Model G "Forecar", a 61-inch twin with front-mounted luggage box – a sort of back-to-front precursor of the Servi-Car.

By this time, the engine was almost unrecognizable in its internal details from the original twin. Relatively exotic alloy steels were employed in high-stress areas of the engine, such as chrome vanadium steel for the "I" beam connecting rods, while roller and ball crankshaft bearings were widely used. A separate three-quart (2.8 litre) tank held oil for the total-loss lubrication system (used oil was either burnt by the engine or drained by hand from the crankcases). Like most contemporary engines, there was no oil pump: good old gravity and flailing engine parts moved the oil around the engine's internals and all the major bearings were of "self-lubricating" phosphor bronze. An auxiliary hand-operated oil pump had become standard in 1912, crudely metering about 25 "drops" of oil per minute.

Until this time, all Harleys had been single-speed, but in 1914 the Model 10F and Forecar debuted the two-speed rear hub. This astonishingly intricate device comprised no fewer than five bevel gears, yet was replaced by a true three-speed gearbox after only one year.

A measure of the twins' success is that, by 1915 the Harley-Davidson range comprised just two single-cylinder roadsters but six twins, including the three-speed Model K "Stripped Stock" –

■ A B O V E *By the time this twin was built in 1917, three-speed transmission was available for an extra $25.*

■ A B O V E R I G H T *The cam drive is clear in this sectioned F-head twin.*

a race replica for its time. Among six "Speciality" twins were the even hotter "Fast Motor" K12 and out-and-out racers such as the KRH. This elaboration continued throughout the 61-inch F-head's astonishingly long career.

So comprehensive was its evolution that, by the time it was discontinued in 1929, almost no part from the original twin would fit.

■ L E F T *An exquisite 1916 board-racing twin. Note the Bosch magneto and single carburettor.*

■ B E L O W *The timing side of a 1917 twin. Note valve-gear cutaways in tank.*

MODEL W SPORT TWIN, 1919–22

One of Harley-Davidson's most radical machines appeared as early as 1919. Developed during the war years and first shown to the public in 1918, the Model W "Sport Twin" was quite unlike the general expectation of what a Milwaukee twin should be. Its cylinders, rather than being tucked close together in a 45 degree V, were set 180 degrees apart. This was Harley's Boxer twin – but unlike BMW's more modern Boxers, this carried its cylinders fore-and-aft like contemporary British Douglas machines.

In theory, this somewhat unwieldy layout should have made the bike very long, but in practice the new model's wheelbase was actually three inches shorter than that of the existing V-twin – just 53½in (1,360mm). It was also low overall and carried its heaviest components in particular low to the ground – a considerable bonus on the rough roads of the time. It also weighed fully 100lbs (45kg) less than its sibling V-twins. Aesthetically, too, the "Brewster Green" Sport looked low and lean, with an elegance of line rarely achieved by previous V-twins. The engine's horizontally-opposed cylinders bestowed perfect primary balance,

■ LEFT *The very Model W machine that set the Three Flag record, riding from Canada to Mexico in less than 75 hours.*

SPECIFICATIONS

Engine	horizontally-opposed side-valve twin
Capacity	35.6 cu in (584cc)
Transmission	3-speed
Wheelbase	53½in (1,360mm)
Top speed	around 50mph (80kph)

making it far smoother than the other big Vs in the Harley range. In fact, this was a most civilized mount all round.

As well as the standard equipment of magneto ignition and gas lights (fed by acetylene gas produced "on the move" by dissolving calcium carbide in water), optional equipment included coil

ignition and true electric lighting. Engine lubrication was taken care of by an automatic pump, freeing the rider from the obligation of injecting just the right amount of oil at just the right time. The three-speed transmission was driven by a multi-plate clutch (albeit hand-operated) running in engine oil, just like a modern motorcycle.

The Sport's drive chain, enclosed in a steel case and lubricated by oil mist from the crankcase breather, was as close to zero-maintenance as chain transmission could get at the time. All in all, the Model W was a neat, light, economical and innovative piece of kit which Milwaukee clearly hoped would find a ready market, as riders were less disposed to the rougher pleasures of previous big twins.

■ LEFT AND ABOVE *It may look ratty, but it still works. The horizontal cylinders and low overall lines of this original Sport Twin are clear.*

Unfortunately the Sport had one major shortcoming – cubic inches, or the lack of them. It was way down on power compared to the existing 61-inch Harley V-twin and similar offerings from Indian. with a displacement of just 35.6cu in (584cc). To compensate, at least in part, it had to be revved hard – indeed it was reputed (very dubiously) to be the highest-revving internal combustion of its time. Yet even when thrashed, power was poor, with a top speed of little more than 50mph (80kph). Then, as now, America's motorcyclists demanded less revs and far more guts. Although its agility made it modestly popular for a while on Europe's more tortuous roads (almost one third of exports to Britain in 1919 were Sport Twins), the Model W was never a success at home. Production ceased in 1922, after just four years on the Milwaukee line.

■ ABOVE *Little can the builders of machines like the Sport Twin have realized the cultural tide they were unleashing.*

MODEL JD & FD BIG TWINS, 1921–9

Milwaukee's first 74-inch model, the so-called "Superpowered Twin" hit America's streets for the 1921 model year. Producing some 18 horsepower, the big engine was intended to compete with Indian's big twins and four cylinder models from Henderson and others. The "74" followed the practice of the "61" from which it evolved, employing inlet-over-exhaust valves (the F-head layout) driven by a single camshaft in a timing cover on the right side of the engine.

However, many major components – crankcases, cylinders and heads – were all new, and both bore and stroke were increased. The transmission was three-speed, the gears and shafts being located in a separate aluminium housing which was connected by enclosed chain to the left end of the crankshaft.

An "automatic" oil pump delivered lubrication for the engine's mixture of plain phosphor bronze, roller and ball bearings. As with almost every other motorcycle of the time, used oil was burned or dripped on to the ground. The multi-plate clutch, on the other hand, ran dry.

■ ABOVE *Sidecars, such as this mated to a Model J, were huge business.*

■ BELOW *An immaculately restored 1928 Model JD, one of the first to feature a front brake.*

Although often referred to generically as the JD, up to 1925 the 74-inch twin might more helpfully be called the Model D, with the addition of essentially the same prefixes as contemporary 61-inch twins. "JD" indicated a complete electrically equipped version, while the magneto model was designated "FD". Where fitted, electrical equipment comprised a six-volt generator, battery, contact breaker points and coil, headlight, tail light and oil

SPECIFICATIONS 74-INCH SUPERPOWERED TWIN	
Engine	F-head V-twin
Capacity	74.2cu in (1,216cc)
Transmission	3-speed
Power	18bhp
Wheelbase	59½in (1,510mm)
Top speed	around 75mph (120kph)

■ RIGHT AND BELOW *This 1925 61-inch twin retains the original olive green colours with maroon and gold pin-striping, unlike the eye-catching example below.*

warning indicator light. An additional "S" in the model description indicated a sidecar model, with lower gearing and a 0.12in- (3mm-) thick steel spacer between cylinder and crankcase mouth to reduce the compression ratio. Other subsequent suffixes included such variables as piston material – A for aluminium, B for iron. The lighter weight and improved heat dissipation of the aluminium alloy pistons were particularly beneficial after their introduction in 1924.

A tubular steel, single-loop frame tied the whole thing together, the rider cushioned from the worst road shocks by a "Full-Floteing" Mesinger saddle. Front suspension comprised similar double-sprung girder forks to the smaller twin. Only a rear brake – a 7¼in (186mm) drum actuated by a long steel rod from a pedal on the right footboard – was fitted until 1928 when a front drum brake also became standard. For markets in which a second brake was mandated by law, an additional "stopper" – essentially a parking brake – could also be fitted. Other changes over the "74"'s life span included the use of "Alemite" surfaces for all chassis bearings in 1924. The rider would periodically inject these with grease from a purpose-made high-pressure grease gun, which did much to

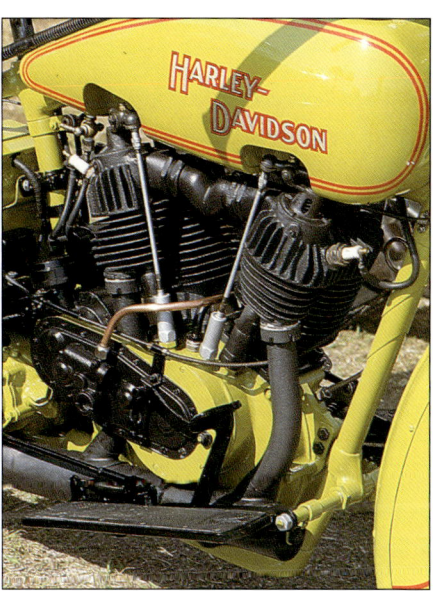

■ BELOW LEFT AND RIGHT *A lower frame carrying a teardrop-style tank first appeared in 1925, whilst front brakes finally arrived for the 1928 model year. The example below left clearly has neither.*

extend component life, especially in wet or dusty conditions. Less practical, but carrying echoes into the styling of Harleys today, 1926 found the big twin equipped with broad "balloon" tyres and a curvaceous "teardrop" fuel tank.

Over its eight-year career, the "74" proved itself a brisk performer which enhanced Milwaukee's reputation for building dependable motorcycles.

Some indication of its virtues – and not least of Harley's tradition of sticking with what worked – was that, at 87 x 101.6mm, the "74"'s cylinder dimensions remained almost unchanged up to the Shovelhead models of relatively recent times.

Clearly, the machine that would take its place in the future would have to be at least as special as the present one. Yet to begin with, at least, it would be anything but.

JH, JDH Two-Cam, 1928-9

Twin-cam and even eight-valve machines had formed the cutting edge of Harley-Davidson's official racing efforts since the First World War, yet the ordinary road-going motorcyclist could only dream of such performance. All that changed in 1928 when Harley offered a two-cam motorcycle to the general public at an affordable price. These special J-series machines were available for two years only, as the 61-inch JH and the awesome 74-inch JDH, which were priced at $360 and $370 respectively.

"The magic words 'two-cam' mean exceptional speed and power," extolled contemporary advertisements, with some justification. Not for the last time, Milwaukee was treading the fine line between effective salesmanship and encouraging public disquiet over bad boys on antisocial machines.

Both twin-cam engines featured inlet-over-exhaust valve operation driven by paired, gear-driven cams in a timing case on the right side of the engine. Instead of operating via Harley-Davidson's customary roller arms, the

SPECIFICATIONS	
Engine	2-cam, F-head V-twin
Capacity	60.33cu in (988cc) or 74.2 cu in (1,216cc)
Transmission	3-speed
Wheelbase	60in (1,525mm)
Top speed	around 85mph (137kph)

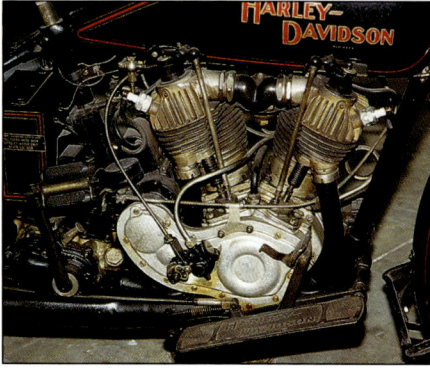

cam lobes acted directly on tappets, offering more accurate valve control, higher revs and improved combustion. The height of each cylinder's inlet valve necessitated flamboyant clearance cutaways in the narrow fuel tank, which gave the "JH" its characteristically racy appearance.

The two engines differed in both bore and stroke, as well as in the use of Dow metal pistons, but were built on essentially the same crankcases. These were connected by roller primary chain to a multi-plate dry clutch and three-speed gearbox, which in turn drove the rear wheel by chain.

As well as the choice of capacities, two specifications of the Two-Cam were offered, although numerous racing specials would be created in private hands. As well as the competitive potential of stripped-down Model Js, Juneau Avenue anticipated a demand for an exclusive road version – or "superbike" as it might be known today. Thus the Two-Cam was available with full electrical equipment, carburettor air cleaner, fully valanced mudguards and front and rear brakes.

Echoes of the machine's racing pedigree were retained, however, in the slimline "sport" chassis, single seat and racer-style two-gallon (7.5 litre) fuel tank.

Even as a roadster, the Two-Cam was billed as "the fastest model ever offered by Harley-Davidson" with the JDH specially recommended "for greatest speed and maximum performance."

With an 80-inch version available on special order in 1929, this olive green projectile was no less than the American equivalent of Brough Superior's sensational SS100 in Europe.

Yet even this degree of exclusivity was priced too high for an American market more interested in cars, and the Two-Cams passed into legend after spending a very short two years in the Harley-Davidson range.

■ BELOW *Reflected glory: an Evo-engined Low Rider basks in the setting sun.*

45-INCH TWIN, 1929–51

One of the most enduring motorcycles in Harley-Davidson's history was announced in October 1927, hitting the road just over 12 months later. The Model D, as it was first styled, was the first of a new generation of side-valve "flathead" V-twins – far cheaper to create than the relatively complex F-head engines. Not much more than a pair of 21-inch "Ricardo" singles on a common bottom-end, it featured three-speed transmission and a spindly frame almost identical to the little single's.

If the beginnings were lacklustre, improvements came fast. Within a year, the "45" benefited from a sturdy new frame with lower saddle but increased ground clearance. It was now available in four guises: D (low compression solo), DS (sidecar), DL (high compression Sport Solo) and DLD Special Sport Solo. Two years later, it emerged from a comprehensive redesign as the Model R. This included aluminium pistons in place of Dow metal (with magnesium offered as a special option from 1933), new crankcases with improved oiling and a sturdier frame.

■ LEFT *An early Model D "45". The unfinned timing cover is one obvious difference from the later Model W.*

SPECIFICATIONS:
1929 MODEL DL

Engine	side-valve V-twin
Capacity	45.3cu in (742cc)
Transmission	3-speed
Power	around 22bhp
Weight	395lbs (179kg)
Wheelbase	56½in (1,435mm)
Top speed	around 65mph (105kph)

In 1933, of course, the Depression was at its deepest. A sign of these cash-strapped times was that this much-improved machine now cost just $280 – $10 less than the Model D had at its introduction. After a further steady regime of continuous improvement, the "45" was transformed once again to become the Model W in 1937. Although the most obvious difference was the adoption of styling from the Knucklehead released the previous year, there were numerous engine

■ LEFT AND RIGHT *The inspiration for the "flathead" nickname is obvious (left). Note the streamlined instrument console, which remains a Milwaukee hallmark.*

improvements as well, with its troublesome crankcase oiling and breathing system getting the lion's share of attention.

The range now comprised not only standard (W), sidecar (WS), Sport (WL) and Special Sport (WLD) models, but also the WLDR Competition Sport Special, a mean-looking stripped-down racer – though by 1941, the WLDR machine was a "Special Sport" roadster, the racer being known by a simple "WR". Four-speed transmission, adopted from the bigger twins, appeared in 1938 and by 1940 the WLA Army version was on the books. By now, the

WLD and WLDR versions carried light alloy cylinder heads with more fin area and a larger carburettor, improvements that would not reach the base models for another five years.

Indeed, the engine would receive almost no more significant changes during the WL's final decade – a far cry from the 1930s when anything from 15 to 30 modifications were made each year. Instead, Harley-Davidson directed its efforts into its overhead-valve models, confining the "45" mainly to cosmetic revisions, partly inspired by the Hydra-Glide. Civilian production of "45"s ceased after 1951, although some

military versions were produced later, and the same side-valve engine would continue to power the Servi-Car into the 1970s. The WL is – and was for most of its life – a crude, heavy machine better suited to the American Prairies or war-torn battlefields than any road with bends. By the time it went out of production, it was a motorcycling dinosaur. Though it was slow, outdated and cumbersome, it was also strong as an ox and almost indestructible: this model had proved itself to be a tough old Hog that for more than two decades had dependably delivered the bacon for Harley-Davidson.

■ OPPOSITE BOTTOM LEFT AND RIGHT *Art-deco influences are clear in the styling of these two striking WL45s. The inspiration for modern Springers is clear in the girder forks, especially on the chrome-plated example on the right.*

■ LEFT *A 1942 WL45, one of the last pre-war civilian models. The "Boat-tail" rear fender appeared in 1939.*

74-inch Side-Valve Twin, 1930–48
80-inch Side-Valve Twin, 1935–41

Far from being the dependable machine the market required, the model which propelled Harley's big-inch fortunes into the troubled 1930s was even more bothersome than that very first V-twin of 20 years earlier. Launched just in time to see the New York stock exchange collapse in 1929, the Model V "Big Twin" began life as a fiasco.

With the original twin, valvegear was the problem. With this new 74-inch model it was almost the entire machine. As William H. Davidson recalled: "bad engine... bad clutch... flywheels too small... frames broke... mufflers became so clogged the engine lost power."

It's a mystery now – and probably was for Harley at the time – why the first of this line were so very poor. The cylinder heads, though now of side-valve layout, retained the proven "Ricardo" pattern of the earlier single.

At 87.3 x 101.6mm, the bore and stroke dimensions were unchanged from the Model D. As before, a single dependable Schebler carburettor metered fuel via a forked manifold. Testing showed that power was up 15 per cent on the old "74".

SPECIFICATIONS: 74-INCH (80-INCH) TWIN

Engine	side-valve V-twin
Capacity	74.2cu in/1,216cc (78.9cu in/1,293cc)
Transmission	3-speed (4-speed from 1937)
Wheelbase	60in (1,525mm)
Top speed	up to 90mph (145kph)

There were novelties, of course, but nothing suggesting the trouble to come. Primary drive was now based on duplex chain, far stronger than the single chain used previously. Revisions to the oil-circulation system promised the rider a less oil-soaked time, as did full enclosure of the valvegear, which was impracticable on the old ioe twin. Other improvements that ought to have been welcomed by serious users included interchangeable quick-release wheels (at a time when punctures were a

■ ABOVE *The mighty VL, the top of the Milwaukee range before the arrival of the Knucklehead.*

■ LEFT *A 1936 VLH 80-inch twin. The spring shield on the girder forks was new for that particular year.*

■ ABOVE LEFT *Hand gear-change would remain a Milwaukee norm until the 1950s. The foot pedal operates this VL's "suicide" clutch.*

■ ABOVE RIGHT *A drab army 74-inch twin. Note the metric engine capacity in the "1200" on the tank.*

NAME GAMES

Not for the first time, Harley-Davidson's model nomenclature looks confusing viewed from decades distant. Sometimes called the "VL", the 74-incher was available from the outset as a straight Model V, with "VL" representing the high compression version, "VS" the sidecar puller and "VC" signifying the use of nickel iron rather than light alloy pistons. This continued until 1934, when options included the VLD ("Special Sport solo" with TNT motor), VD (low compression, solo), VDS (low compression, sidecar gears) and VFDS (heavy duty commercial, TNT motor). In 1935, the 80-inch model appeared and was dubbed VLDD (Sport solo) or VDDS (sidecar), alongside existing 74-inch models. This all changed for the 1937 model year, with "U" replacing "V" (alphabetically backwards). From then on, all the big side-valve twins' model designations began "U-" (80-inch models were indicated by a subsequent "H"). Thus a simple "U" indicated the basic 74-inch model and the plain "UH" was the equivalent 80-inch model.

daily hazard) and an improved electrical system with better weather protection. The frame, too, was new: lower, heavier and reputedly sturdier than before.

For a company trading on unsurpassable reliability, the "74"s problems were serious indeed. No matter how handsome the new

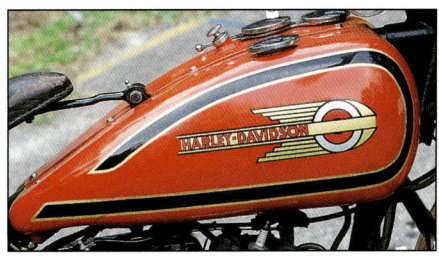

■ ABOVE AND BELOW *With the change to four-speed transmissions in 1937, the Model V became the Model U, one year before this handsome 80-incher was built. Note the revised timing cover.*

machine was, dressed in olive green with red pin-striping, no-one would buy it if it didn't work. To its credit, Milwaukee dropped everything to fix all the faults and the Model V proved dependable for the rest of its days.

Having benefited from the fixes applied to the 74-inch model, the 80-inch model released for 1935 proved almost completely problem-free. The bigger engine was substantially similar to the contemporary "74", the extra capacity resulting from an increase in stroke from 101.6 to 108mm.

For 1937, the V-series gave way to the U-series big twins, with four-speed transmission, improved engine oiling and both the running gear and styling from Knucklehead twins. Both were capable of up to 90mph (145kph), had vestigial brakes and no rear suspension. Production of the "80" effectively ceased after 1941.

WLA & XA

■ LEFT *The redoubtable WLA. Note the large auxiliary air-cleaner to prevent the motor choking in dusty conditions.*

■ WLA, 1940–5

If the Willys Jeep was the archetypal American military four-wheeler during the Second World War then Harley-Davidson's rugged old 45-inch flathead twin was its two-wheeled equivalent. By the time the United States entered the war in December 1941, the "45" had proved itself during a dozen years of civilian development and was the obvious choice for an army workhorse. The first example, dubbed WLA (the A stood for "army") appeared in 1940 and was initially scarcely more than a drab green WL. By 1941, it had acquired blacked-out auxiliary lights, an oil-bath air-cleaner (intended for North African conditions) and a quieter fishtail exhaust. Depending on the precise military requirements, luggage racks were added, front and rear, plus a gun scabbard and under-sump bash plate.

That pivotal year also brought the first of around 18,000 WLC models built for the Canadian military, which differed principally in having a foot-operated gear change on the right, rather than hand-change on the left. Anti-hertz suppressors and more comprehensive

blackout gear were added later, and by late 1943 – the year in which WLA/WLC production peaked, at over 27,000 – even the crankcases were painted olive drab. Each machine bore a plate warning the rider not to exceed 65mph (105kph), not that the WLA was capable of very much more. Of around

■ BELOW LEFT AND RIGHT *The key to the WLA's success was its low-tuned, dependable engine, which had already enjoyed over a dozen years of development since the original Model D of 1929. Later examples had slotted "black-out" lights.*

SPECIFICATIONS: WLA	
Engine	side-valve V-twin
Capacity	45.3cu in (742cc)
Transmission	4-speed
Power	around 22bhp
Weight	varied with specification
Wheelbase	59½in (1,510mm)
Top speed	limited to 65mph (105kph)

■ LEFT *Although American-liveried models are best known, over half of military WL production went to other countries' armies.*

SPECIFICATIONS: XA

Engine	side-valve horizontally-opposed twin
Capacity	45.1cu in (739cc)
Transmission	4-speed
Power	around 25bhp
Wheelbase	59½in (1,510mm)
Top speed	around 65 mph (105kph)

■ **LEFT** *Most observers would fail to recognize this as Milwaukee iron: the horizontally-opposed XA twin.*

88,000 WLs produced for war-time service, many went to Russia, of which later examples were specified WSR models. It is reputed that some 30,000 Red Army Harley-Davidsons entered Berlin as the war in Europe drew to a close. Milwaukee's contribution to the war effort was marked by no fewer than three Army/Navy "E" awards for excellence in military production – although this was to backfire commercially on the company when thousands of WLAs were sold as war surplus after 1945, damping-down the post-war recovery.

■ XA, 1942–3

Although Milwaukee built some military versions of the 74-inch side-valve twin (UA) and even fewer ELC Knuckleheads for the Canadian forces, the factory's second-string army model was the curious XA. Powered by a horizontally-opposed 45.1cu in (739cc) twin with shaft final drive and plunger rear suspension, the XA was expressly

■ **BELOW** *Note the shaft drive coupling and large air-cleaner on this flathead XA.*

■ **BOTTOM LEFT** *Although most XAs were intended for North African use, this example is painted in non-desert livery.*

■ **BOTTOM RIGHT** *Note the instruction plate: the military ensured that as little as possible was left to chance.*

designed for use in the North African desert. The transmission was four-speed, with foot change and twin carburettors feeding the two side-valve cylinder heads. This may seem reminiscent of contemporary BMWs: this was a direct copy of the German machine. Juneau Avenue did not copy the opposition's dependability, for it reputedly suffered serious bearing failures due to the Sahara's heat and sand. As a result, only around 1,000 XAs were built, all during the years 1942–3, though this may have been because the North African campaign was drawing to a close. There was also a rare XS variant with sidecar. A civilian prototype derivative of the XA was tested during 1946 but failed to reach production.

MODEL K, 1952–6

If a single model demonstrated Milwaukee's problems during the post-war years, it was surely the Model K, unveiled in November 1951. Virtually a technological throwback, the "K" was born into an age when competition from Europe was intensifying almost monthly. Opposition machines offered high-performance overhead-valve engines with 100mph- (161kph) plus performance and the finest chassis ever built. In response, Harley-Davidson offered as its premier model an antiquated, long-stroke, side-valve twin as its premier sports model, which struggled to reach 80mph (129kph).

Advertised as "America's Most Sensational Motorcycle", the "K" was "designed to outperform, outride, outlook, outvalue ... any motorcycle in its class." Of course, this was only true if a class existed for absurdly slow and out-dated machines – which it might if Milwaukee's plea for a 40 per cent tariff on imported motorcycles had succeeded in May 1951. Harley literature claimed 30 horsepower for the Model K, only a little less than the contemporary 650cc Triumph Thunderbird. Whether true or not, the V-twin was no match for the

SPECIFICATIONS	
Engine	side-valve V-twin
Capacity	45.3cu in (742cc)
Transmission	4-speed
Peak power	30bhp
Wheelbase	60in (1,525mm)
Top speed	around 80mph (130kph)

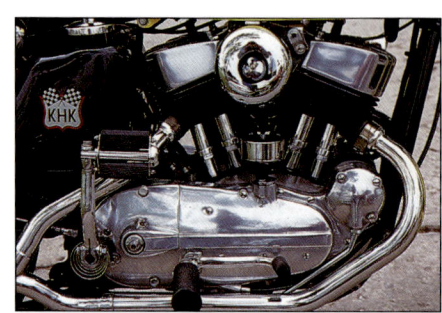

■ TOP *Aided by a 30.5cu in (500cc) limit for ohv engines, the side-valve 45.3cu in (742cc) Model K fared better on the track than on the street.*

103mph (166kph) Britisher. Yet remarkably, Joe Leonard became first American national champion in 1954, on a machine substantially derived from the K. Its other saving grace was that it was the only large-capacity motorcycle Hollywood stars could be insured to ride – in other words, the K was so slow, it was considered safe.

True, the K was the first Harley-Davidson twin to feature suspension at both ends: "easy riding" double-action telescopic forks up front with a swinging-fork rear end (oddly, a sprung seat was retained.) By the standards of Triumph, BSA and Norton in particular, the handling was ponderous and mushy, although the eight-inch (200mm) brakes weren't bad for the time. It offered a hand-operated clutch and in a demonstration of supreme optimism, its speedometer was graduated to 120mph (193kph).

Nor was the K dependable, at least initially, as it was beset by a variety of performance and reliability problems. Perhaps the worst was its habit of breaking its "large, rugged" transmission gears, until a switch to forged parts after 1954. In many other respects, the bike was sturdy and sensibly conceived, such as in the use of taper-roller bearings for the swing-arm pivots. Bore and stroke were identical to the WL's: 70 x 97mm. The four-cam, air-cooled engine enjoyed generous finning to its aluminium heads and iron

■ ABOVE AND LEFT *The best of the breed: a KHK in strident yellow.*

barrels, and it featured in-unit construction of engine and gearbox, with triplex chain drive, long before this became widespread among competitors.

Some years after the age of the K, Harley revealed what many had suspected – that it was only a stop-gap model to see the company through until something better could be developed. Although history records that the Model K was superseded by the Sportster, something more radical was envisaged originally. The familiar 45-degree V layout was dropped in favour of a wider 60-degree engine to be known as the KL, with "high" cams, twin carburettors and side-by-side rather than forked connecting rods. This would have increased secondary vibration, although the wider V angle would have gone some way to reducing primary imbalance.

Evidently, the KL project ran into patent conflicts with Vincent and ran out of development time, although it is possible that the progress of European machines convinced Harley that something even more potent was required. By way of a stop-gap to the

stop-gap, a drastic 19mm increase in stroke raised the Model K's capacity to 55cu in (883cc) for 1954, and power to a claimed 38bhp, in an attempt to stay at least within sight of the Brits. The cover of *The Enthusiast* showed one Elvis Aaron Presley on board just such a machine in 1956, by which time work on the model's successor was already well in hand. As well as the basic KH, a tuned Super Sport Solo KHK model with high-lift camshafts, polished ports,

leaner styling and lower handlebars arrived in 1955. Though they were ostensibly intended for racing, most found their way on to America's streets where they proved far more acceptable to American sports riders – their top speed exceeded 90mph (145kph). After 1956, the old flathead expired and was replaced by the first of the overhead-valve Sportsters. As the KR and KRTT, it soldiered on for more than a decade as Milwaukee's principal racing iron.

■ TOP *Pictured here is a handsome example of a 1956 Model K.*

■ LEFT *The K probably looked cooler than it went, especially here at Daytona Beach, Florida.*

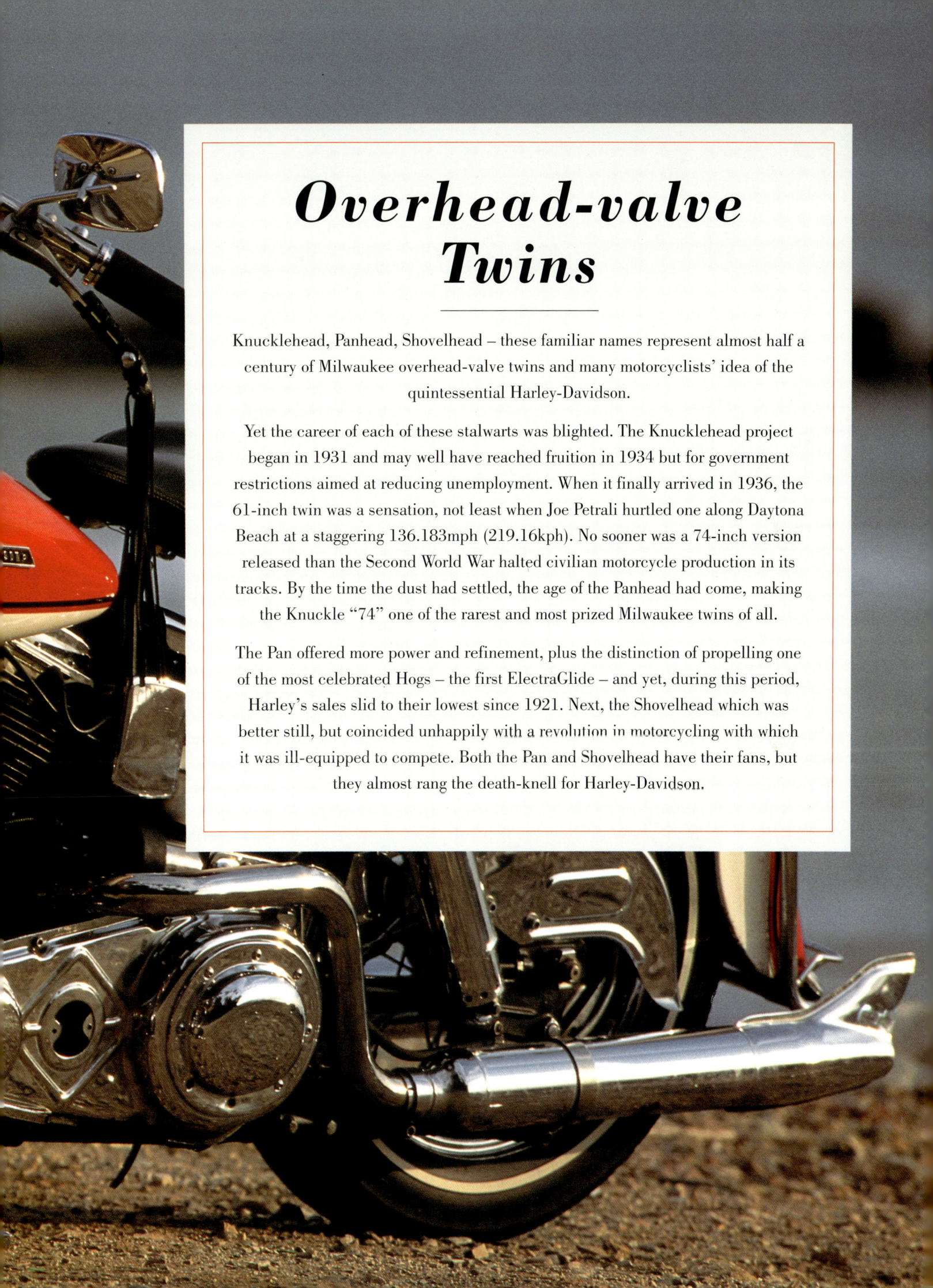

Overhead-valve Twins

Knucklehead, Panhead, Shovelhead – these familiar names represent almost half a century of Milwaukee overhead-valve twins and many motorcyclists' idea of the quintessential Harley-Davidson.

Yet the career of each of these stalwarts was blighted. The Knucklehead project began in 1931 and may well have reached fruition in 1934 but for government restrictions aimed at reducing unemployment. When it finally arrived in 1936, the 61-inch twin was a sensation, not least when Joe Petrali hurtled one along Daytona Beach at a staggering 136.183mph (219.16kph). No sooner was a 74-inch version released than the Second World War halted civilian motorcycle production in its tracks. By the time the dust had settled, the age of the Panhead had come, making the Knuckle "74" one of the rarest and most prized Milwaukee twins of all.

The Pan offered more power and refinement, plus the distinction of propelling one of the most celebrated Hogs – the first ElectraGlide – and yet, during this period, Harley's sales slid to their lowest since 1921. Next, the Shovelhead which was better still, but coincided unhappily with a revolution in motorcycling with which it was ill-equipped to compete. Both the Pan and Shovelhead have their fans, but they almost rang the death-knell for Harley-Davidson.

KNUCKLEHEAD, 1936–47

It's difficult to appreciate the impact Harley-Davidson's first overhead-valve roadster twin must have had on a motorcycling public that was emerging groggily from six long years of Depression. In fact, no Milwaukee model before or since was ever quite so comprehensively new. Even the latest Twin Cam, remember, is installed in largely familiar running gear.

Not so with the legendary Knuckle. Not only was the engine a major departure, but it sat in an equally new twin-cradle frame, with just the mudguards and generator remaining from the flathead VL. Its striking styling owed much to the art-deco innovations of the Depression years, capped by a teardrop-style tank, complete with an audacious white-faced Stewart-Warner speedometer calibrated to 120mph (193kph). Fanciful, perhaps, but factory

■ LEFT *The overhead-valve Knuckle was the biggest development in years*

■ ABOVE *Milwaukee makes metal come alive.*

■ BELOW *This 1946 FL Knucklehead looks better now than it did when new.*

SPECIFICATIONS

Engine	ohv V-twin
Capacity	60.32 or 73.66cu in (989 or 1,207cc)
Transmission	4-speed, hand change
Power	40 or 45bhp
Weight	565lbs (256kg)
Wheelbase	59½in (1,510mm)
Top speed	up to 90mph (145kph)

■ LEFT AND BELOW *A finned timing cover (left) identifies this as a post-1941 Knucklehead. Compare this with the "smooth case" example below. A host of other changes also came in for 1942.*

testers had reported 100mph (161kph) during development. Little wonder that would-be owners queued in droves when the first examples were shipped to dealers in January 1936, despite the $380 Knuckle costing $40 more than a contemporary 80-inch twin.

Designed by William S. Harley and Lothar A. Doerner (the latter tragically killed while testing a 1937 model), the 60.32cu in (989cc) twin underwent no fewer than 70,000 hours of testing, according to contemporary claims. As with previous mainstream models, the Knuckle was initially available in three guises: E (standard, discontinued after 1937 but restored during the Second World War), ES (sidecar) and EL (high-compression sport). All proved free-revving and eager, while the EL in particular – with 40 horsepower at 4,800rpm – offered a huge performance increase over the laggard side-valvers. Even the mighty 80-inch VL couldn't come close to an ohv twin.

Yet despite the time-consuming route to production – and not for the first time – there were initial problems.

Many changes were implemented during the first year of production, including frame reinforcing and revisions to the kick-start gears. The rocker assemblies

became enclosed for 1938, by which time the patented tank-mounted instruments also included warning lights for low oil pressure and generator output.

But the 61's worst fault concerned its dry-sump lubrication. Some parts got too little oil while others – including the road underneath – got too much. A partial fix was introduced in 1937 but the glitch was not completely solved

until the arrival of the centrifugally-controlled oil pump bypass of the 74-inch (Model F) Knuckle of 1941. The crankshaft main bearings had been up-rated in 1940, perhaps in anticipation of the extra loads on the bigger engine. The arrival of the more potent "74" also brought larger 8½in (216mm) diameter flywheels, revised crankcases, an up-rated seven-plate clutch and a carburettor choke increased to 1⅛in (28.6mm). By now, the two ohv models combined were comfortably out-selling Milwaukee's established range of side-valve twins. Given further development, the Knuckle could surely have become better still, but with the outbreak of war in December 1941, production concentrated almost exclusively on military side-valve twins and development of the ohv models all but ceased.

Milwaukee lore has it that the very best of the big Knuckles were those built in that final pre-war year, but hostilities meant that relatively few Model Fs reached the road until 1947, when the line's reign was almost over.

Not surprisingly, that first overhead-valve "74" remains one of the most prized Harley roadsters of all.

By 1948, however, a new pretender was on the scene: the age of the Panhead had arrived. At last it was goodbye, finally, to oil leaks from the rocker box, which was a problem that had never been completely solved on the Knucklehead.

HydraGlide, 1949–57

■ BELOW RIGHT *Although the Panhead shared its bottom-end with the Knuckle, the heads, valve-gear and oil feeds were new.*

■ BOTTOM *The HydraGlide name came from the bike's new telescopic front forks, then becoming widespread on motorcycles worldwide.*

For the 1948 model year, Harley-Davidson had unveiled its new Panhead engine, mating it to a revised "Wishbone" frame with characteristic "dog-leg" front downtubes. Within a year, it had been eclipsed by the first of Milwaukee's "Glide" models.

Although retaining a rigid rear end, the HydraGlide broke with the company's usual reliance on leading-link sprung forks. Instead, here was a Hog with a modern oil-damped telescopic front-end. As if to compensate for this fit of novelty, the Hydra persevered with a uniquely American hand-change gearbox until 1952 and even later as an option for true die-hards.

For the present, however, it was as close to modern as heavyweight Harleys would get. Billed with characteristic restraint as "the nearest thing to flying and as modern as a spaceship," the first HydraGlide was, in truth, only a relatively slight departure from the model that went before.

SPECIFICATIONS	
Engine	ohv V-twin
Capacity	60.32 or 73.66cu in (989 or 1,207cc)
Transmission	4-speed, hand change
Power	around 50/55bhp
Weight	560lbs (254kg)
Wheelbase	59½in (1,510mm)
Top speed	around 95mph (152kph)

As was company tradition, a host of detail changes would follow year-on-year. Many of these would be cosmetic (the speedometer alone received an astonishing degree of attention), but most concerned the internal workings of the engine and chassis, making the final HydraGlide of 1957 very different from the first. It should be remembered, however, that in the American automotive industry in general, the 1950s and 1960s were characterized much more by developments in styling than in functional engineering.

In essence, the Panhead engine comprised new cylinders and heads grafted on to the Knucklehead bottom end. The heads were now aluminium with hydraulic valve lifters (tappets), and internal oilways had replaced the Knuckle's external lines.

Like the Knucklehead it replaced, this new Panhead was produced in both 61- and 74-inch (989 and 1,207cc) versions, designated models E and F respectively. Six versions comprised the initial range: Model F Sport Solo, FL Special Sport Solo and FS Sidecar twin, with the designations repeated for the 61-inch motor. All featured four-speed transmission, while sidecar models had lower gearing and reduced compression ratios. At their launch, all sprung-fork Model Es cost $635, with the larger engine adding a mere $15 to the price. Within a year, the introduction of the HydraGlide had upped those figures by precisely $100. Just to be on the safe side, sprung-fork models – designated ELP and FLP – remained in the range for one transitional year.

Of literally hundreds of detail changes, the first major improvement came in 1950 when revised cylinder

■ BELOW *Add electric start and rear shock absorbers and you'd have an ElectraGlide. The real thing was to take another 17 years.*

■ BELOW *White tassels probably weren't around when the HydraGlide was king of the road, but whitewall tyres certainly were.*

heads with larger ports added a claimed ten per cent more power. The 61-inch Model E was dropped for 1953, by which time annual sales of the smaller Panhead had slumped to below 1,000. The same year – the company's fiftieth anniversary – brought about Harley-Davidson's familiar "mid-series" bottom-end redesign. This included major changes to both crankcase halves as well as the relocation of the hydraulic lifters from top to bottom of the pushrods. A new "straight-leg" frame was brought in for 1954, followed by the FLH Super Sport model (the "H" stood for "hot") 12 months later, with gas-flowed heads and 8:1 compression ratios.

Even the FLH was no tyre-shredder, though, retaining the low-revving, high-torque virtues of every Milwaukee V-twin. These were very much machines in the American tradition, having ponderous steering, limited ground clearance, marginal brakes and hand gear change.

In terms of styling, the HydraGlide was pure 1950s – or perhaps pure 1990s, since so many modern Harley models echo its visual themes. Central to this was its low-slung profile with "Air-Flow" front and rear fenders (mudguards).

A chrome-plated tubular steel front "safety guard" was offered as an option from 1950, with "HydraGlide" emblems available one year later – both mimicking those gracing the very latest FLs.

It had some early "innovations" – like black silencers and fork sliders – that did not last, but overall the Hydra-Glide made an impact that is still very much with us today.

■ LEFT *Yes, this 1953 HydraGlide could almost be a year 2000 Softail. That's precisely the point of Retro-Tech.*

FL DUOGLIDE, 1958–64

By 1958, Harley-Davidson was already in grave difficulties as annual sales hovered around a paltry 12,000 under intense competition from European machines. To make matters worse, the start of the Japanese invasion was just one year away – though no-one knew it at the time – with the arrival of Honda into the American market.

One way in which the company responded was through increased diversification of its range – first the Model K, and then the Sportsters took different directions from the heavyweight twins. But by the late 1950s, the latter – the FL models – were woefully outdated and badly in need of a major overhaul. Instead, they got little more than a facelift.

After the HydraGlide, the DuoGlide was the logical next step. As well as real, oil-damped telescopic front suspension, the Duo floated on a swinging-arm rear end, hence the name. This was a major improvement on the face of it, even though the Model K had beaten it comfortably for the distinction of being the first Harley-Davidson twin

SPECIFICATIONS	
Engine	ohv V-twin
Capacity	74cu in (1,207cc)
Transmission	4-speed
Power	55bhp
Weight	575lb (261kg)
Wheelbase	60in (1,525mm)
Top speed	around 95mph (152kph)

with rear suspension. By the time it appeared in 1958, however, pretty much everything it offered had already been done – and done better – by every other major motorcycle manufacturer, with the exception of the Duo's hydraulic rear brake. Unfortunately this was little more than a gimmicky novelty, since both hubs contain tiny, ineffective single-leading shoe drums.

With major engine revisions having been implemented in 1953 and in 1956, the DuoGlide's engine might as well have been called the "Panhead Mark

II". It also benefited from more generous finning than previous Pans for 1958, as well as an up-rated generator. With the 61-inch Pan long departed, all DuoGlides enjoyed 74-inch (1,207cc) power. The range offered a choice of hand or foot gear-change and Sport or Super Sport ("H") tune, making four models in all. In 1958, the hotter specification added $65 to the standard $1,255 purchase price.

Central to the machine's layout was a new "Step-down" frame with larger diameter backbone and attachment

■ ABOVE *The distinctive speedometer is original; the handbag is not.*

■ LEFT *The chrome crash bars, fender rails and panniers were available as part of 16 Harley-Davidson option groups.*

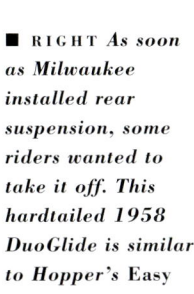

■ RIGHT *As soon as Milwaukee installed rear suspension, some riders wanted to take it off. This hardtailed 1958 DuoGlide is similar to Hopper's Easy Rider mount.*

■ BELOW *An original 1961 example shows how Harley intended it to look.*

points for the twin rear shock absorbers. These incorporated oil-damping (typical of the time, for rebound only) and their springs were enclosed in gleaming chrome-plated shrouds. The new frame necessitated many other modifications – to the oil tank, toolbox and fork yokes – although the first Duos looked rather like soft-tailed HydraGlides.

If the Duo's looks weren't enough for aspiring owners, 1958 also introduced a huge expansion in the number of factory "option packs" including no fewer than nine for the new DuoGlide. These comprised accessories groups for "Chrome Finish", "Road Cruiser" and

"King of the Highway", with a bewildering array of lights, luggage items and other paraphernalia. The "King of the Highway" package included front and rear nudge bars, twin rear lights and a dual exhaust system.

Unfortunately it didn't sell very well, being particularly unsuited to most export markets, although it accounted for around 40 per cent of Milwaukee's sales at home. The Duo didn't much like corners, and was woefully under-braked. Even the "H"-designated Super Sports models, with optional high-lift camshaft and higher

compression pistons, weren't rapid. Vibration was intense at high engine speeds, leaving much of their potential power unused most of the time, except by the most determined riders – who would probably seek the high-rev thrills of a Triumph Thunderbird anyway.

Then, as now, the DuoGlide was about a different sort of motorcycling, with its big, slow-revving engine and charismatic looks. It was indisputably a Harley, with all the attributes and vices of the breed. And it was also indisputably beautiful.

FL ELECTRA-GLIDE, 1965

Of all Harley-Davidson models, surely the enduring FL ElectraGlide is the one that best epitomizes the breed. The "FL" designation actually arrived with the first 74-inch Knucklehead of 1942 and has since been ever-present in the Milwaukee range. The model that has carried those laurels with the greatest distinction has been the thundering ElectraGlide – the quintessential model since its 1965 debut.

Yet for all its lusty pedigree, that first ElectraGlide was little more than a DuoGlide with the addition of 12-volt electrics and an electric starter which – initially, at least – did not prove altogether very dependable.

Just as there was a 12-month hiatus between the introduction of the Panhead and the HydraGlide, Harley-Davidson waited until 1966 before giving the Glide something new. From its second year of production, it was powered by the new Shovelhead mill with its (relatively) more efficient "Power-Pac"

■ ABOVE *The first of the breed, the 1965 ElectraGlide. The large battery box distinguishes it from earlier DuoGlide.*

heads. Initial examples used the alloy-headed Panhead engine which had first appeared in 1948 and gone on to propel the first Glide (the HydraGlide of 1949) and the DuoGlide of a decade later. The Hydra- had been the first big twin with telescopic forks while the Duo- added swinging arm rear suspension.

The starter motor itself lived behind the rear cylinder and engaged on the rear of the primary drive. The DuoGlide frame had to be opened up slightly to accommodate it, yet still there was no room for the earlier model's tool kit. Surprisingly for a unit "borrowed" from an outboard motor, the first starters were

SPECIFICATIONS: 1965–1970	
Engine	ohv V-twin
Capacity	73.66cu in (1,207cc)
Transmission	4-speed
Power	around 55bhp
Weight	595lbs (270kg)
Wheelbase	60in (1,525mm)
Top speed	95mph (152kph)

■ ABOVE LEFT *It would do considerably more than 12mph (20kph), but in Harley-land style counted as much as numeracy.*

■ LEFT *For little more than $1,500, this Milwaukee dream could be yours – in 1965.*

■ RIGHT *As leaps forward go, the ElectraGlide was conservative: both hand-change and foot-change versions were available until 1972.*

■ BELOW *The last of the Panheads: in 1970 the Shovelhead took its place.*

troublesome when damp and the kick start was prudently retained. Harley later adopted Homelite starters, which proved much more reliable.

Like all Harley big twins, the ohv engine ran forked con-rods to eliminate rocking couple (so the rear cylinder was precisely, rather than roughly, masked by the front). Primary drive was by chain to a four-speed box (with a sidecar option, up to 1980, of three forward and one reverse). Capacity was 74cu in (1,207cc): the current 81.74cu in (1,340cc) dimensions didn't arrive until 1970 with the new generation of "alternator" Shovelheads. The rest was almost unchanged from the DuoGlide, complete with five-inch (127mm) whitewall tyres and running boards, although for the first time a five-gallon (19-litre) "Turnpike" tank was fitted. Of

the four-model range, two versions retained hand gear change, which would remain an option until 1972.

In short, this was never a state-of-the-art machine. Indeed the "King of the Road" touring pack offered in 1966 required the rear shock absorbers to be relocated forwards, to the detriment of the Glide's handling, which had already proved to be rather pedestrian.

For all that, it's a strikingly handsome machine – one which looks far better than it performs. Like most Harleys, the rear brake is good but, prior to the arrival of a front disc in 1971, no prudent rider would choose to stop a Glide in a hurry.

This is a device for getting into top gear and staying there as you cruise serenely to the next horizon.

FX SuperGlide, 1971–84

In the late 1960s, customizing was king. In California in particular, Harley-Davidson owners were tearing their machines to pieces, discarding one piece and adding another to produce unique examples of what were to become known as "blend" bikes. Nowhere was this more publicly demonstrated than in the film *Easy Rider*, with Peter Fonda cruising to New Orleans on the outrageous "Captain America" alongside Dennis Hopper's hardtailed DuoGlide.

Milwaukee's response was as startling as it was controversial. When the SuperGlide was unveiled for the 1971 model year, it was the first example of a genre quickly dubbed "factory custom". The influential *Cycle* magazine's misgivings were typical.

"Is the American motorcyclist ready to ride around on someone else's expression of personal, radical tastes?" it asked, before testing the newcomer and answering its own question enthusiastically in the affirmative. Such was the SuperGlide's impact that almost every major motorcycle manufacturer has since produced its own interpretation of the "factory" custom – invariably to less

■ LEFT *By the 1970s, customs were all the rage. Willie G.'s official version was less flamboyant than this "Captain America", but its impact was more enduring.*

■ BELOW LEFT *Part Sportster, part FL, the SuperGlide was an instant hit, with 4,700 built in the first year.*

effect than Harley's original. From a modern perspective, taking into account models such as the Springer Softail, the FX wasn't actually all that radical. Styled and conceived by Willie G. Davidson, it was essentially a combination of heavyweight FLH frame, 74-inch Shovelhead engine (which still carried "FLH" on the timing cover) and running gear, with the front end from the existing XLH Sportster. The rear end's styling was dominated by a fibreglass boat-tail stepped seat and integral rear mudguard which had debuted as an option on the Sportsters the previous year. Although widely viewed as a defining element of the model, this lasted for only one year and was quickly replaced by a more conventional rear mudguard.

Compared to the FLH, the SuperGlide also had pegs in place of footboards, with foot controls revised to suit. Both exhausts were low-level feeding paired silencers on the right hand side. Wheels were 19in (483mm) front, 16in (406mm) rear, both equipped with fairly feeble drum brakes. The 3½ gallon (13 litre) fuel tank included a built-in speedometer. Functionally, it was a far from perfect machine, although it went and handled far better than the FLH

■ BELOW *In 1974 the SuperGlide gave rise to the FXE. Twin discs first appeared for 1979.*

■ BOTTOM *Although the SuperGlide's most eye-catching feature, the "boat-tail" rear end was an option rather than standard equipment.*

■ BELOW *A later, disc-braked FX. Note the "AMF" logo on its tank.*

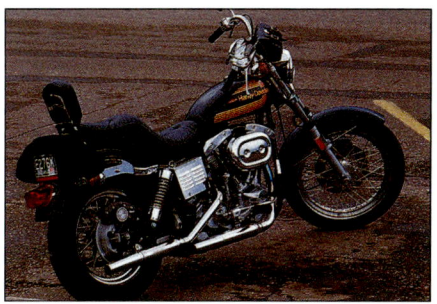

SPECIFICATIONS: 1971–80	
Engine	ohv V-twin
Capacity	73.66cu.in (1,207cc)
Transmission	4-speed
Power	around 60bhp @ 5400rpm
Weight	590lbs (267kg)
Wheelbase	61in (1,550mm)
Top speed	105mph (169kph)

from which it was derived, not least because it was more than 66lbs (30kg) lighter. The hybrid instantly struck a chord and sold well – 4,700 units in its first year, almost as many as the established FLH ElectraGlide. After two years, it acquired hydraulic disc brakes at both ends and improved suspension with stiffer springs. A year later, an electric start option, the FXE, was added. Japanese Showa forks were added in 1977, electronic ignition in 1978 and twin front discs in 1979, before it developed 80-inch Shovelhead power for 1981. For the final year of production in 1984, five-speed transmission was added; the FXR and FXRS Super Glide II models were also on the Milwaukee stocks, comfortably out-selling the old stager. Although almost two decades would pass from the SuperGlide's launch to the turnaround in the company's economic fortunes, it's impossible to overstate the effect the model has had on Harley-Davidson's affairs. The FX invented the concept of the factory custom and led to landmark models such as the FXEF Fat Bob in 1979 and Sturgis 12 months later.

FXS LOW RIDER, 1977–85

These days, the Low Rider range is as essentially Harley-Davidson as the Sportsters and heavyweight Glides, yet it wasn't until 1977 that Willie G. brought us the first Low Rider model. The FXS Low Rider was, in essence, another reworking of the seminal Super Glide theme, which in turn was to spawn yet another dynasty of Milwaukee hardware.

Described as "one mean machine" in Harley-Davidson's own publicity, the FXS was a new type of custom cruising model, intended to be as content cruising wide-open prairies as downtown avenues. It was finished in menacing gunmetal grey with flat, drag-style handlebars on pulled-back risers, resonating echoes of the choppers that countless enthusiasts had created in the past. The laid-back name came from a seat height of just 27in (686mm), a characteristic which would appear again in the Huggers of the future.

Although the 80-inch Shovelhead first appeared on the FLH ElectraGlide in the Low Rider's debut year, the FXS was initially powered by the established 74-inch Shovel. The engine came

SPECIFICATIONS	
Engine	ohv V-twin
Capacity	73.7cu in (1,207cc)
Transmission	4-speed
Power	60bhp
Weight	550lb (249kg)
Wheelbase	63in (1,600mm)
Top speed	98mph (158kph)

finished in crinkle black paint with highly polished outer covers. Both exhaust pipes curved back along the right side below a new "1200" air-cleaner cover, before thumping the atmosphere through a single chromed muffler. The revised frame was heavily raked and fitted with highway pegs, allowing the rider to stretch out, like the latter-day *Easy Rider* the styling sought to emulate.

Chassis components included Japanese Showa telescopic forks, chromed twin rear shock absorbers and dual

front disc brakes. Sadly, the stoppers were still disconcertingly feeble in their effect, although the rear was relatively fierce with massive leverage available at the pedal. The puny forks, too, were prone to flex while the short-travel rear suspension units were at the same time

■ LEFT *The FXS-1200 Low Rider was described as "one mean machine" when it first came on to the scene.*

■ BELOW *This 1985 FXRS Custom picks up the tradition of V-Twin power that was started by the Knucklehead, Panhead and Shovelhead.*

both harsh and under-damped. It would be a while before any heavyweight Harley aspired to even the sketchiest handling prowess.

Quicksilver handling, though, wasn't what the FXS was all about. The model was an instant success, hitting the public's wish-list almost as soon as it was unveiled. It was comfortably out-selling the SuperGlide by its second year, with almost 10,000 examples built. Clearly, the Low Rider concept was here to stay and the breed has benefited from a steady stream of improvements in

every succeeding year. Along the way, they've spawned eye-catching sister models, such as the 80-inch FXB Sturgis of 1980 – the year after the FXS itself was first offered with the larger Shovelhead mill.

The biggest novelty came in 1983 with the much revised FXSB Low Rider. The "B" represented the adoption of the Aramid-fibre toothed belts first seen on the Sturgis for both primary and secondary drive.

A small number of late-1984 examples may have received the new 80-inch Evolution motor, but it wasn't

until the FXRS "Custom Sport" Low Rider of 1985 that this much-improved engine became widespread. By the time five-speed transmission was grafted on to the same model 12 months later, the modern Low Rider series had arrived.

■ ABOVE AND LEFT *The FXS caught on almost instantly, becoming Milwaukee's best-selling model by 1978.*

■ BELOW *Although built in 1992, this Low Rider Sport displays features similar to the original FXS.*

FLT TourGlide, 1980

Like most things Harley-Davidson, the TourGlide didn't suddenly appear out of the Milwaukee ether, it just sort of evolved. One fundamental element, the 80-inch Shovelhead engine – a long-stroke derivative of the old "74" – first appeared on the 1978 FLH Electra-Glide. Another arrived one year later with the FLH Classic, offered as standard with special paint and wheels as well as a complete set of "Tour Pak" touring extras. The Tour Pak was ultimately to become the heavyweight long-haul norm, comprising saddlebags, luggage rack, "batwing" fairing and chromed crash bars.

In 1980, Harley bundled the two together, adding a few other choice ingredients for good measure, and the FLT TourGlide was born. The most obvious change was the replacement of the ElectraGlide's handlebar-mounted fairing with a bigger, more protective frame-mounted fairing, now equipped with twin headlights. There was an improved new frame with "sport bike"

SPECIFICATIONS	
Engine	ohv V-twin
Capacity	81.6cu in (1,338cc)
Transmission	5-speed
Power	65bhp
Weight	765lb (347kg)
Wheelbase	62½in (1,590mm)
Top speed	100mph (161kph)

■ LEFT *Additional long-distance kit allowed heavyweights such as this late-1970s ElectraGlide to evolve into the TourGlide series.*

■ RIGHT *In 1981 the FLTC Classic arrived, to be followed by further Tour-Glide variations.*

geometry and a box-section backbone. Fabricated from both tubes and forgings, the frame was further modified at the rear to increase suspension travel. At the front, it now extended forward of the head-stock for more secure fairing mounting.

Less obvious – unless you were riding one – were a host of engine improvements also bestowed on the FLT. Rather than existing separately, the engine and transmission were now bolted rigidly together, gaining the benefits of unit construction without the drawbacks. The transmission itself was now five-speed for the first time on any big twin Harley-Davidson roadster, permitting even more long-legged gearing than before. A new Motorola electronic ignition virtually guaranteed dependable running at all engine speeds (or perhaps not: within a year it gave way to the superior V-Fire II system).

Final drive was still by roller chain but now fully-enclosed in its own oil-bath, a useful asset on any long-distance machines. Chain was superseded by a toothed belt drive on the FLTC Classic of 1984, which became standard across the FL range the following year.

Despite some initial scepticism, the Aramid fibre belts – made from a similar material to that used in bullet-proof vests – had worked well on the lighter V-twins, lasting four times as long as a chain, at similar cost but without the mess. By 1993, they would be a welcome feature on every Harley-Davidson model.

If that particular virtue was still in the future, an equally compelling one first appeared on the inaugural TourGlide. In contrast to previous rigidly-mounted engines, for the first time the FLT engine was installed using a clever three-point rubber-mounting system

designed to isolate the rider from the worst of the big V-twin's vibration. In essence it couldn't be simpler, but the effect transformed the machine, making it smoother and more usable than any previous big twin.

Anyone with $6,013 to spare in 1980 could buy what was undoubtedly the smoothest, most comfortable and lavishly-equipped motorcycle

Milwaukee had ever produced, a machine tailor-made for demolishing large distances.

The TourGlide might not be everyone's idea of motorcycling but it launched a generation of Milwaukee luxury tourers to which rival manufacturers have yet again paid the ultimate compliment: most of them have since tried to copy it.

■ LEFT *All Tour-Glides enjoyed five-speed transmission and rubber engine mounts. The Evo powerplant brought further refinement from 1984.*

Sportsters

If the original Model K was behind the times, the machine that superseded it has become a legend. Launched in 1957, the 883cc XL Sportster was a much finer machine in every respect. Where the Model K was a flathead, the Sportster featured overhead valves. The engine and gearbox were now in-unit (a refinement to which Harley beat much of its opposition) and there was full swing-arm rear suspension with car-type shock absorbers, allowing early Sportsters to be sold as suitable for both on- or off-road use. The XL was an instant hit, accounting for one fifth of Harley-Davidson's total production in its first year on sale.

As well as meeting performance expectations, the Sportster also looked the business. Its lean, purposeful lines, capped with a minimalist fuel tank and raucous "shorty" exhausts are little changed even today.

Having learned its lesson with the Model K, Milwaukee didn't stand still with its new Sportster, introducing improvements year on year. The first electric-start model was brought in for 1967, more power in 1968 and more again with the first 1,000cc version of 1972, culminating in the delicious XR1000 of 1983. By the time Evolution-engined models arrived in 1986, there was a choice of either 883cc or 1,100cc engines, the latter eventually growing to 1,200cc.

THE FIRST OF THE BREED

After the debacle of the side-valve Model K, the Sportster series roared across America like a refreshing gale. At its heart was an overhead-valve engine displacing the same 883cc as the XLs of today. In those days, however, both the cylinder barrels and heads were of heavy cast iron, the latter with a hemispherical combustion chamber.

Each valve had its own gear-driven camshaft, operating the valve via "High Speed Racing" roller tappets and solid push-rods. A single Linkert carburettor fed mixture into the cylinder, where shallow domed pistons offered a compression ratio of 7.5:1. In 1957, peak power was around 40bhp but this rose considerably with the ported, high-compression "H" and "CH" versions, reputedly reaching 58bhp at 6,800rpm by the mid-1960s. By then, a good one could exceed 110mph (177kph).

Cosmetically, even fully-equipped versions of the XL were as lean as motorcycles can be – an attribute most retain to this day. Not so much as a pillion seat was permitted to mar their purposeful lines. The chassis was adequate if altogether less persuasive. A

■ RIGHT *In 1957 the first of the Sportsters proved to be a giant leap forward from the primitive side-valve Model K.*

SPECIFICATIONS: XL SPORTSTER 1957

Engine	ohv V-twin
Capacity	883cc
Transmission	4-speed
Power	40bhp
Weight	438lbs (199kg)
Wheelbase	58.5in (1,485mm)
Top speed	95mph (152kph)

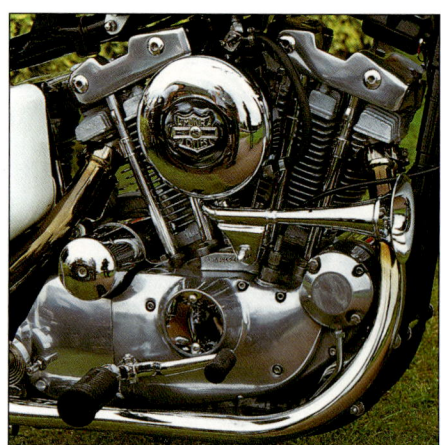

■ ABOVE RIGHT *The mercurial "H" stood for high-compression and was intended to signify that this machine was hot.*

■ BELOW *By 1970, the Honda CB750 had arrived, yet the XL had feeble brakes and relatively lacklustre performance.*

combination tubular steel and cast iron frame married "easy riding" telescopic forks and twin rear shock absorbers, with the swing arm pivoting on taper roller bearings. Each 18in (457mm) wheel held an underwhelming eight-inch (200mm) drum with shoes one inch (25mm) wide.

In truth, the handling wasn't great, although (for a Harley) the Sportster was light and low enough for a good rider to manhandle it into shape. An improved front fork helped matters from 1968 but the XL only really began to behave with the appearance of a lighter and stiffer frame, universally praised in press road tests, in 1982. By this time, the old one was very much feeling its age. Those first Sportsters were comparable with almost anything on the road and, at $1,103 apiece, sold like "Competition Hot-cakes". By the late 1960s, this was comfortably Harley's best-selling range.

■ LEFT *The XLCH, which is commonly dubbed "Competition Hot". Sportsters remain the only Harleys to use unit construction engines.*

■ SPORTSTER EVOLUTION

Since its introduction in 1957, the XL Sportster has been the bread and butter of the Harley-Davidson range. Within a year, the stock Sporty had been joined by the high-compression XLH Sportster Sport, the legendary XLCH "Competition Hot" (as it is commonly called, although it actually meant "Competition High-compression") and the stripped-down XLC Sportster Racing. Perhaps surprisingly, the latter, intended for off-road use, lasted for only one year.

Originally marked for a life on dirt, the XLCH featured the 1.8 gallon (8.2 litre) "peanut" tank (standard was 3.5 gallon /16 litres), big valves,

magneto ignition – and neither lights, speedometer nor battery. It was superseded by a fully road-equipped XLCH one year later. Detail changes included a switch to 12-volt electronics in 1965, two years before the first Sportster electric start – or "Push the button... ZAP... and away you go" as Milwaukee promoted it.

For 1971, the previous dry clutch gave way to a wet one. The first 1,000cc examples were the XLH/XLCH Super H and Super CH of 1972, the extra displacement coming from a 4.5mm increase in bore size to offer around 60bhp. (The captivating XLCR and XR1000 are dealt with in

detail later.) Another spin-off from the Sportster line was a series of hybrid models, hoping to hit any untapped market niche. The XLT Touring came out in 1977, equipped with saddlebags, high bars and a thicker seat. More than 1,000 were built in the first year, a mere six in the second, giving way two years later to the XLS Roadster, with extended forks, highway pegs and a 16in (406mm) rear wheel. That year might be remembered as the last year of the legendary XLCH. A lasting hybrid was the optional Hugger package of 1980, offering shorter shocks and a thinner seat – this was a precursor of the true Hugger models of today. The equally far-reaching XLX61 came out in 1983, a stripped-down, budget-priced version of the XLH1000 aimed at cash-strapped riders. It has been Milwaukee policy ever since to produce a cut-price "entry-level" model. When the 883 and 1,100cc Evolution models arrived for 1986, it was to be the beginning of a new chapter in the Sportster story.

■ LEFT *The very first of the Sportsters, from 1957. The Model S-inspired fuel tank came later.*

XLCR CAFE RACER, 1977–8

If black truly is beautiful, then the XLCR was sublime. So dark, it practically drank in the light, the Café Racer was another of Willie G. Davidson's variations on an old theme, in this case re-working the basic 1,000cc Sportster which had first appeared in 1972. When it arrived for the 1977 model year, the XLCR looked revolutionary – the most unashamedly different Harley-Davidson yet.

At its heart was the then biggest XL engine grafted into a redesigned frame, with extended rear frame rails allowing more vertical shock absorbers than before. Most striking of all was the "Black-on-Black" paint job. This included gloss black bodywork, crinkle-black engine finish and a black Siamesed exhaust which snaked together below the air-filter housing – which, naturally, was black.

The 3.8 gallon (14.5 litre) fuel tank – black, of course – was unique to the XLCR, as were a fibreglass "bikini" fairing and single seat. The latter ended with a

■ ABOVE *The stylish XLCR, with its "race replica" footrests, did not produce the kind of sales that Harley had hoped for.*

racing-style "bum stop" – although a dual seat option was available for 1978, the model's second and final year of manufacture. Cast aluminium Morris wheels, as well as rear-set "race replica" footrests and controls, were also provided as standard.

The move to more vertical shock absorbers was a not particularly successful attempt to improve the Sportster's habitually sloppy handling.

At the same time, twin hydraulic front discs were fitted in much-needed pursuit of improved braking. They proved moderately powerful, if rather lacking in feel.

SPECIFICATIONS

Engine	ohv V-twin
Capacity	992cc
Transmission	4-speed
Power	around 60bhp
Weight	540lbs (245kg)
Wheelbase	58.5in (1,485mm)
Top speed	110mph (177kph)

■ BELOW *In truth the XLCR looked better than it went.*

25mph (40kph) slower than rival sports machines, with equally inferior handling and braking. Worse still, the XLCR bore all the worst hallmarks of the AMF years. Contemporary road tests might praise the marque's "indefinable magic" but they would equally slate the Café Racer (and its siblings) for being "appallingly built and hideously unreliable," to which was usually added "prohibitively expensive".

By the end of the model's brief reign, Harley-Davidson's share of the American motorcycle market had slumped to a paltry four per cent, yet it would be several years before the reborn company would seriously set about tackling its manufacturing shortcomings. This wasn't specifically the fault of the XLCR, of which just 3,124 examples were built, but this model did illustrate Harley-Davidson's problem – that beauty had to be much more than skin-deep.

Visually, this "top Sportster" was superb. True, it wasn't to everyone's taste, but most bikers would cast admiring glances at this stylish symphony in black. For all its eye-grabbing credentials, however, the XLCR was far from a runaway success.

On the one hand, most Harley die-hards found it visually too radical. On the other hand, more neutral buyers found sport-bike image and performance far more effectively packaged in Japanese and Italian machines. For all that, the XLCR is a desirable classic now, though at the time it was neither a vintage Harley-Davidson model nor a competent sports machine.

With around 60bhp and a top speed close to around 110mph (177kph), the XLCR was certainly no slug, but the bald truth was that it went at least

XR1000 Sportster, 1983–4

Unveiled at Daytona in March 1983, the XR1000 was the closest Harley-Davidson fans would ever get to a road-going XR racer. Even this far on, it's still many people's idea of the ultimate Harley Sportster. This should have come as no surprise because the big XR roadster was designed (and the prototype built) in the official factory race shop under the direction of Dick O'Brien. The 1000 could scarcely have enjoyed a better pedigree – O'Brien had managed Harley-Davidson's racing efforts since 1957 and overseen every moment of the XR750's career. Fittingly, O'Brien retired in the same year as the XR1000 roadster was released, making it an appropriately snarling swansong.

The $6,995 1000 wasn't quite a big-bore factory racer with lights but it was pretty special all the same. The engine employed a normal Sportster bottom end capped by special cylinder barrels, heads, fuel and exhaust systems. The aluminium heads were based on those of the racing

SPECIFICATIONS:	
Engine	ohv V-twin
Capacity	998cc
Transmission	4-speed
Power	70bhp
Weight	487lbs (221kg)
Wheelbase	59.3in (1,505mm)
Top speed	115mph (185kph)

■ ABOVE *Not quite a racing XR750 for the road, but visually the XR1000 came pretty close.*

XR, each reputedly shipped to Los Angeles to be ported and polished by legendary tuner, Jerry Branch (although it's likely that Branch simply oversaw the work, since a total of 1,777 XR1000s were built).

Induction was in the capable hands of twin 1½in (36mm) Dell'Orto carburettors with accelerator pumps, each breathing through huge, free-flowing K&N air filters stacked, flat-track style, on the engine's right side. Although stock Sportster camshafts were employed, valve-lash was adjusted by

■ RIGHT *Possibly the most prized of all AMF-era models, the XR1000 was race boss Dick O'Brien's major contribution to Harley roadsters.*

■ RIGHT *This example has been customized to superb effect with a flat-track style rear mudguard and seat.*

■ BELOW RIGHT *That's better: the same colours flown by Jay Springsteen, Scott Parker and the rest of the champion racers.*

racer-style eccentric rocker shafts. The push-rods, too, were special lightweight alloy components. Lumpy pistons gave a 9:1 compression ratio. Paired high level black megaphone exhausts growled back along the machine's left side.

This bespoke engine was red-lined at 6,200rpm but there was no earthly need to spin it that high, since the spread of power was immense.

Peak power – a claimed 70bhp – arrived at 5,600rpm but the engine pulled strongly from as few as 2,000rpm. Maximum torque was 48lb/ft (65Nm) at just 4,400rpm. The speedometer was calibrated only to 110mph (177kph), a figure a good XR could reach comfortably.

With optional performance kits offering more than 90bhp, the sky was almost the limit.

In truth, the XR's chassis was far less impressive than its engine. The frame and running gear were based on the XLX61, which was also new for 1983,

with a nine-spoke, cast 19in (483mm) front wheel and 16in (406mm) rear. Rear suspension was in the hands of twin shock absorbers of no great quality, adjustable only for spring pre-load. Travel was quite short and the action

harsh, making the XR nervous when ridden hard on bumpy surfaces. The brakes, however – twin 11½in (292mm) front discs – were surely the best Harley-Davidson had put on any roadster model up to that time and improved even further for 1984.

During the model's second year, it was offered with optional black and orange "factory" racing paintwork as well as the original steel grey. This seemed to be a suitably fitting livery for such a great machine.

The XR1000's reign as the ultimate sporting Harley-Davidson ever to have been produced by Milwaukee came to an end when production of this model ceased in 1984.

XLH883, 1986– PRESENT

With a price tag of just under $4,000 when introduced as the XLX61 in 1983, the basic Sportster was precisely the type of entry-level machine so conspicuously absent from the Harley-Davidson stables in the past. This was a piece of genuine Milwaukee hardware at a price almost anyone could afford. In 1986, the deal was made even better with the appearance of Evolution engines across the Sportster range and the arrival of the XLH883. Then, just 12 months after that, would-be 883 owners got an even more irresistible package with the announcement of Harley's innovative buy-back scheme: "Trade in your XLH against an FX or FL within two years and we'll guarantee $3,995 on your old machine." How could anyone lose?

The smallest Sportster was the last model to benefit from the wave of refinements sweeping through the Milwaukee range. But in two short years from 1992, Harley-Davidson's bargain-basement superbike progressed from being the runt of the Harley-Davidson litter to become a thoroughly competent

SPECIFICATIONS

Engine	ohv V-twin
Capacity	883cc
Transmission	5-speed
Power	52bhp
Weight	489lb (222kg)
Wheelbase	60.2in (1,530mm)
Top Speed	103mph (166kph)

■ BELOW LEFT *No frills, no tassels and bereft of baubles, the 883 is the most honest-to-goodness model in the Milwaukee range.*

■ BELOW RIGHT *The least expensive, lightest and easiest Harley to handle is popular with male and female riders alike.*

machine. There were dozens of detail changes over those two seasons, but two stand out. First came five-speed transmission for 1992, followed 12 months later by belt final drive.

The extra gear transformed the smallest Harley from a relatively buzzy, busy machine into a far more laid-back device, with the bonus of a better gear-shift. The tooth-belt drive made it smoother still, with the added benefits of low maintenance and cleanliness.

The first belts – pioneered by Harley-Davidson and the Gates company that manufactures them – aroused a degree of suspicion. However, thanks to space-age Aramid fibre reinforcement (similar to Kevlar) they last at least four times as long as a chain, cost about the same and are practically unknown to fail. This was to make the XLH slightly more of what it was always good at – being a lean, spare and handsome means of filling practically all the space between headstock and rear spindle. There are no tassels, no gratuitously shiny but ultimately useless bits – just plain, single-seated function.

Of course, like all Harleys, the function in question has relatively little to do with sheer speed, handling or stopping. The 883 is essentially a cut-down cruiser, its low-profile Hugger stablemates all the more so. It looks cool while allowing its rider to appreciate, with as little intervening sanitation as possible, the most intimate doings of the internal-combustion engine.

Peak power from the 883cc engine is around

52bhp at a distinctly unruffled 5,500rpm – 1,000rpm after the arrival of maximum torque of 52lb/ft (70.5Nm). Acceleration is brisk rather than vivid, although the ample torque means there's always power on hand.

This motorcycle might be smaller than any other that Harley has produced, but crank open the throttle at almost any revs and the Sportster lunges forward on the same irrepressible wave of power. Without the rubber-mounting available on some larger models, engine vibration can be intense at high revs. There is no question that the 883 series represents good quality and value.

As well as the basic 883, there's also the

Hugger – a variant dating back to 1979 and so called because it squats even lower to the ground.

They hardly depreciate and, with a bit of care, they can all last practically forever. Best of all, however, more than 40 years after the introduction of the original XL, the 883s continue to embody the same frill-free virtues.

For a chunk of a legend, the 883 really is a steal.

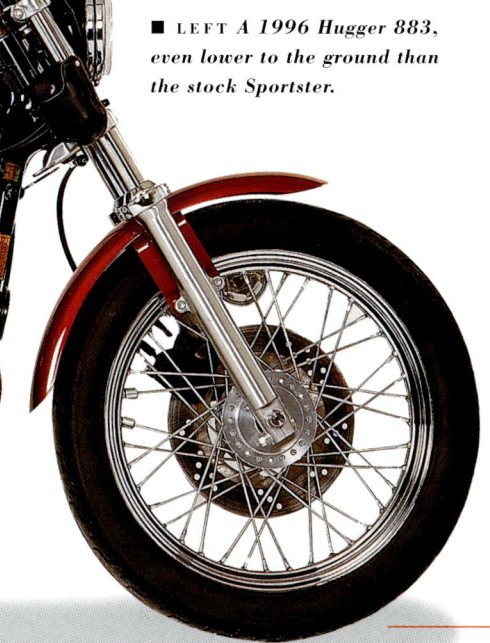

■ LEFT *A 1996 Hugger 883, even lower to the ground than the stock Sportster.*

XL1200S SPORTSTER SPORT, 1996–PRESENT

By the mid-1990s, the redoubtable Sportster family was approaching its fortieth birthday – and beginning to show it. True, Evolution V2 engine technology had reached the old XL steeds on the 883 and 1100 Sportsters for the 1987 model year. Twelve months later, Milwaukee unleashed the first of the family's 1,200cc models, the XLH. Essentially this was the old 1,100 engine with the bore increased from 85.1 to 88.8mm. The stroke remained unchanged at 96.8mm, the same as the 883. Other than a change to five-speed transmissions and belt drive across most of the Sportster family in 1991, the range remained largely unchanged until the appearance of the 1200S in 1996. Along the way, it had definitely lost some of the fire that had burned in the first of the breed all those years before.

Those first Sportster Sports were perhaps a case of "close, but no cigar." Initially, their chief distinction was the adoption of improved, fully-adjustable suspension components at both ends, mated to softer, grippier tyres – but the engine remained stubbornly unmoved.

■ LEFT *Once sorted, the Sportster Sport represented a quantum leap in Harley-Davidson engine power, handling and stopping prowess.*

■ BELOW LEFT *The Sportster Sport was extremely popular, and the 1998 model pictured was long-awaited by its devotees.*

SPECIFICATIONS	
Engine	ohv V-twin
Capacity	1,203cc
Transmission	5-speed
Power	75bhp
Weight	518lbs (235kg)
Wheelbase	60.2in (1,530mm)
Top speed	110mph (177kph)

Sportster fans had to wait another two years before the model truly reached its peak, but the 1998 Sportster Sport was surely worth the delay. In broad terms, the engine was little changed from previous Sportsters, with its hydraulic tappets, dry sump and triple-row primary chain driving a wet multi-plate clutch and toothed-belt final drive. Naturally, the 1200S carries higher overall gearing: 2.103:1 compared to 2.259:1 on the 883.

However, a comprehensive engine revamp had raised torque figures by an average of 15 per cent throughout the twin's 2,000–5,500rpm operating range. The model now had both the chassis and the engine to justify its "Sport" aspirations at last.

Essential to these improvements was an all-new ignition pack igniting not one, but two spark plugs in each cylinder, promoting quicker, more efficient burning of the incoming fuel/air charge. Although a conventional carburettor was retained – a 1½in (40mm) constant velocity Keihin instrument equipped with an "accelerator" pump – combustion control was further improved by an

■ RIGHT *Clean lines are common, but note improved calipers between this early example and the 2000 Sportster that is pictured below.*

electronic management system even more sophisticated than the V Fire III set-up fitted to its sister models. The system, incidentally, also affords high-tech electronic diagnostic capabilities. These measures allowed Harley-Davidson's engineers to bump up compression from 9:1 to 10:1, offering a substantial increase in mid-range power.

As well as lumpier pistons, the revised powerplant benefited from a larger, less restrictive exhaust system and new camshaft design. The camshafts offer both higher lift and longer duration, again with the emphasis on enhancing mid-range torque. Harley can claim a peak torque figure of 78lb/ft (106Nm) at 4,000rpm, over 50 per cent higher than the 883. With not only much improved power characteristics but better throttle response as well, the Sport feels even stronger than the figures might show. The 1200S looks every inch as mean and muscular as a Sportster should, with its clean lines and understated black engine highlights. Nor is this a deception, for the twin-plug Sport package delivers genuine punch. Better still, it stops and handles in a most un-Milwaukee-like manner – a

mantle several more recent models have since adopted, to welcome effect.

In short, this not only proved to be the best XL for years, but perhaps was also the model with which Harley rediscovered the Sportster's roots, and made a great addition to the range.

■ ABOVE LEFT *One of the first examples of the 1200S. Later versions were better.*

■ ABOVE RIGHT *The Sportster is really a joy to ride.*

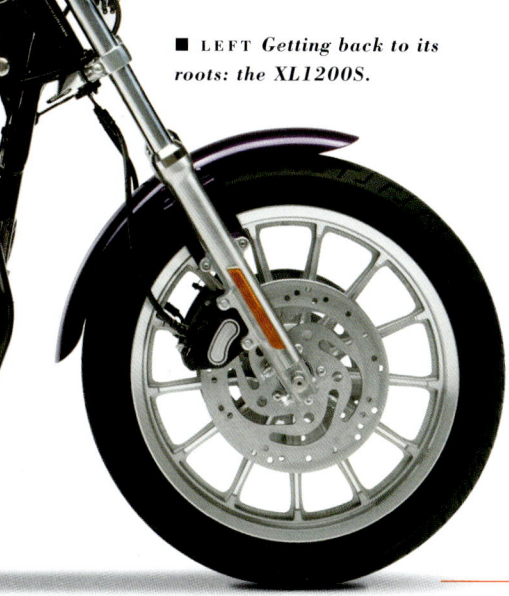

■ LEFT *Getting back to its roots: the XL1200S.*

Softails

It is a typical Harley irony that the Evolution V2 engine, unveiled in 1984, brought about a revolution in the company's fortunes, whereas the Twin Cam engine launched in 1998 was truly revolutionary in engineering terms. Then came the Twin Cam 88 and its balance-shafted brother, the 88B – so revolutionary that it might aptly be dubbed the Revo V2. It took four years and 2.5 million test miles (4 million km) to bring the project to fruition, resulting in an engine with 18 of 450 components in common with the 80-inch Evo motor. The result has as many benefits over its predecessor as the Evo had over the Shovel. If it does half as well Harley-Davidson can look forward with confidence.

If the Evolution V2 engine was a success, then so was the model in which it first appeared. Softails are the glittering style kings of the Harley range, and the first of these was the seminal FXST Softail of 1984. "Retro-Tech" is something modern in concept but executed and styled in a recognisably "classic" way. To achieve the hardtail illusion, Harley-Davidson engineers designed a massive triangulated rear swinging fork, with twin shock absorbers hidden from normal view beneath the engine. The clean overall lines of the machine emphasized the elegant sweep from head stock to rear wheel spindle, heightening the hardtail effect. Visually, however, the origins were the 1949 HydraGlide, the first Harley model with telescopic front forks. If any modern motorcycle belonged outside a 1950s American diner, the Softail was surely it, until the even more eye-grabbing 1988 Springer Softail brought the same throwback concept to the front end as well. Retro-Tech has since established itself as the fourth major theme in the Milwaukee menagerie, alongside the Sportsters, Dynas and Glides. Indeed, of all Harley models, Softails are invariably in the shortest supply.

FXST SOFTAIL, 1984

Certain motorcycles have stood out as memorably special over the years, mobbed for days on end at motorcycle shows. Honda's original CB750F was one, as was Ducati's sensuous 916. In recent years, the Milwaukee equivalent has surely been the first Softail, from 1984. True, all Harley-Davidsons are someone's idea of beauty but the FXST had a quality all its own.

Based on the existing FXWG Wide-Glide – somewhat loosely, to judge by appearances – the Softail had bikers not knowing quite where to look. Did they focus on the all-new Evolution V2 engine or eyeball that strangely elegant rear end? Most probably they did both and Softails are still being eyed covetously to this day.

The Softail's rear suspension was a clever piece of lateral thinking based on an old theme, created for Harley by consulting engineer Bill Davis. The inspiration almost certainly came from custom craftsmen such as Arlen Ness – and even carries a distant echo of the Goudier-Genoud endurance racing Kawasakis. Essentially, it's an inverted cantilever rear end (as per Vincent and

SPECIFICATIONS	
Engine	air-cooled ohv V-twin
Capacity	81.6cu in (1,338cc)
Transmission	4- (later 5-) speed
Power	69bhp
Weight	604lbs (274kg)
Wheelbase	66.3in (1,685mm)
Top speed	106mph (170kph)

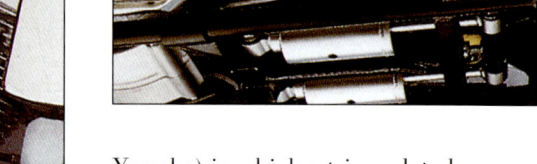

■ TOP RIGHT, CENTRE RIGHT, RIGHT AND ABOVE *The earliest versions of the Softail featured Evo engines with four-speed transmissions, although contemporary FLs enjoyed five speeds. Even a kick start was originally retained.*

Yamaha) in which a triangulated assembly pivots at the top, near the seat, rather than at the usual place. Paired, gas-charged Showa shock absorbers lie unobtrusively under the engine. The layout has little to do with function but a lot to do with style, something it

■ LEFT *With its fake hardtail rear end, the 1984 FXST was the first true "Retro-Tech" model. The series has since become the most stylish and desirable in the range.*

demonstrated superbly. Despite the space constraints inherent in the twin-damper system, Softails in fact boasted more rear suspension travel – 4in (103mm) – than any other models in the Harley range.

Maybe the Softail look wasn't keenly anticipated, since most people didn't know it was coming, but the engine certainly was. Although a few very early 1984 Softails may have been built with Shovelhead engines, every one since has had belt-driven Evo power. With its all-new light alloy top end, the new big twin produced around 70bhp at 5,000rpm and a withering 84lb/ft (114Nm) of torque at just 3,600rpm. Indeed, the spread of power was so immense that almost no-one complained that 1984 examples had to make do with four-speed gearboxes. A five-speed cluster was installed for 1985, by which time a lighter diaphragm spring clutch had also appeared.

The chassis is characterized by an immense 66.3in (1,685mm) wheelbase and a seat height of 1in (25mm) lower than even a Low Rider's seat. Fuel is carried in the familiar, bulbous, two-piece Fat Bob tank, split across the mid-line, with a speedometer set in the

centre. Wheels are wire-spoked, 21in (533mm) front and 16in (406mm) rear, carrying a single hydraulic disc apiece. Unlike contemporary Glides, the 80-inch engine is solidly mounted, although rubber-insulated handlebars and footrests compensate to some extent. Softails may be stylish, but smooth they are not.

The low saddle and forward-mounted "highway" pegs impose an appropriately laid-back riding position. As for

■ **LEFT** *The Softail Custom introduced in 1987 was the first of many models inspired by the original FXST.*

handling: well, the Softail doesn't – it just sort of rumbles from A to B and all the better if that doesn't include too many fast corners. The suspension at both ends is woefully under-damped, the front forks are characteristically soft and woolly, and the rear is, frankly, harsh. Nonetheless, the expansive wheelbase and conservative steering geometry keep things more or less in line. Besides, this is a bike for cruising.

It's a measure of the overall rightness of the concept that, superficially at least, Softails appear little changed to this day. This disguises the vast improvements Harley-Davidson has made in build quality and detailing since the time of the FXST's launch.

Above all, there's the inescapable fact that this inspired piece of post-modern design was a huge and instant success.

Although not the most practical model that Harley-Davidson has ever built, it certainly can be said that Softails are the most eye-catching and, above all, the most prized.

FXSTS SPRINGER SOFTAIL, 1988-PRESENT

In late 1987, the motorcycle world took one look and pinched itself – twice. The Springer Softail unveiled for the 1988 model year looked like no new motorcycle of the previous 40 years. Gone were the telescopic front forks to which we had become accustomed. In their place was a trellis-work of bright-chromed steel members, linkages and springs. It was called "Springer", and was as audacious as it was surreal.

As Harley said at the time, the new front-end wasn't just reborn, it was re-invented. The Springer front end was styled along the lines of the girder forks seen on almost every make of motorcycle from before the 1920s until the late 1940s, but the technology and the detail were all-new. Using computer-aided design (CAD) and the latest materials, Milwaukee had created a system which not only afforded an acceptable level of wheel travel (around

4in/100mm) and suspension control, but which freed its designers to make the styling statement of the year.

We now had Retro-Tech at both ends: Springer at the front to accompany Softail lines at the rear. The engine,

naturally, was the doughty 80-inch Evo, styled for its new role and fitted with staggered shorty dual exhausts.

Like all "conventional" Softail models, the new Springer offered defiantly lazy steering geometry. In this case, a shallow 32-degree steering head gave a generous 5¼in (133mm) of trail. The wheelbase was a lanky 64.6in (1,640mm). Unlike standard Softails, Springers roll on slow-steering 21in (533mm) front wheels, with a 16in (406mm) hoop at the rear. Inevitably, the result isn't quite at the cutting edge of modern suspension performance. Any Softail rear end can be harsh, especially

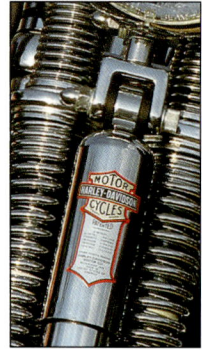

■ ABOVE *A modern damper unit (with Harley sticker) controls the movement of the Springer forks.*

■ LEFT *No-one pretends Springers give state-of-the-art handling, but who needs it on a cruise in the sun?*

SPECIFICATIONS	
Engine	air-cooled ohv V-twin
Capacity	81.6cu in (1,340cc)
Transmission	5-speed
Power	69bhp
Weight	625lbs (284kg)
Wheelbase	64.6in (1,640mm)
Top speed	100mph (161kph)

■ RIGHT *The Springer has always been exclusive. Around 1,350 were produced in its first year, compared to more than 14,000 other Softail models.*

■ BELOW RIGHT *Optional screen, trim and running lights give the owner of this Springer even more to polish.*

■ BOTTOM *Aftermarket fishtail silencers and two-tone paint contrive to make this Springer look for all the world like a 1946 FL.*

over freeway seams, and the latter-day girders lack the control of even Fat Boy's massive telescopic forks. Such judgements miss the point, however. Of all the Milwaukee models, Springers are unashamedly machines for stately cruising – and are as far removed from a Japanese "crotch rocket" as a 1959 Cadillac.

If 1987 marked the Springer's debut, then 1997 marked what many regard as its finest hour. As well as offering practical accessories such as leather saddlebags as standard, the 1997 FLSTS Heritage Springer Softail went

further down the classic road, combining even more vintage styling with today's retro-technology. "Loaded with chrome and leather," publicity material hailed at the time, "the Heritage Springer Softail screams nostalgia." And so it did, from its bright-chromed fishtail mufflers to its deeply-valanced mudguards and whitewall tyres. Even at first glance, the result is sublime, the level of detail extraordinary. Note the nostalgic front fender-tip light and the "retro-1940s tombstone tail-light once commonplace on Harley-Davidsons decades ago." Admire a seat with a leather fringed valance "embossed with a basket-weave pattern and accented with conchos".

The ultimate factory custom had come a long way from the original SuperGlide. As the man said: "Is it a motorcycle or is it art?"

FLSTN Heritage Softail Nostalgia, 1993

Dubbed the "CowGlide" on its release for the 1993 model year, the limited-edition Heritage Nostalgia was the fanciest incarnation of Milwaukee's fanciest line. The nickname came from its hairy, black-and-white natural cowhide seat and saddlebag inserts, but there were plenty more cosmetic tricks where they came from. Little wonder its creators described it as: "Without doubt, the most distinctive-looking motorcycle in Harley's 1993 line ... nostalgic-looking ... but thoroughly modern." It had already proved a winning formula.

Modern, of course, means something else in Harley-Davidson's wondrous time-warp world – like whitewall tyres and forks straight out of the 1940s. Ever since beginning life in 1986, the Heritage Softail package attempted to re-enact the look of the 1949 HydraGlide, with its "hardtail" rear and gleaming metal fork shrouds.

Fine detail isn't something you'd normally expect from a device scaling almost one third of a ton, but this is a Harley, so the tank badge is a specially fired enamel named "jewelled

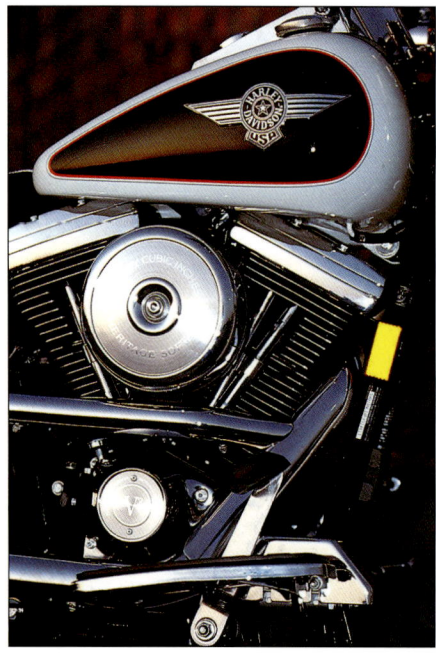

■ ABOVE *The engine was an 80-inch Evo like any other, but the Nostalgia package set it apart.*

■ BELOW *The "CowGlide" was derived from the stock Heritage Softail, here seen cruising in company with a LowRider.*

SPECIFICATIONS	
Engine	air-cooled ohv V-twin
Capacity	81.6cu in (1,340cc)
Transmission	5-speed
Power	69bhp
Weight	710lbs (322kg)
Wheelbase	64.2in (1,630mm)
Top speed	100mph (161kph)

cloisonné." Yet at heart, it's essentially an even more customized variant on the Heritage Softail Classic, available only in Birch White and Black two-tone, with black and chrome engine trim. Power comes from an identical 80-inch Evo engine booming out the same 69bhp at a mere 5,000rpm and a mammoth 70-or-so pound-feet (95Nm) of torque at an even lowlier 3,500rpm. Like the rest of the 1993 range, the Nostalgia benefited from a taller final drive (61-tooth rear pulley) for lower revs at cruising speeds. Improved brake and clutch levers, master cylinder sight glasses and a new, neater engine-breather system also arrived for the same model year.

To ride, it's inevitably much like any other Softail, particularly the Classic or Fat Boy (with which it shares wheel sizes), steering geometry (32-degrees rake, 5.8in/147mm trail), forks, footboards, handlebars and almost every other relevant dimension. The only significant differences are a fuel tank almost ¼ gallon (1 litre) larger and the addition of a hefty 93lbs (42kg) of mass compared to the basic Softail model.

With suspension springing as soft as the CowGlide's considerable weight will allow, handling falls somewhere between sedate and ponderous. Over bumps, the steering is vague and accompanied by a slow weave whenever the road turns lumpy. As with the brakes, it's adequate if it is ridden with prudence.

Since Softail engines are not rubber-mounted, the vibrations intrude towards the top of the rev range even with its higher overall gearing – or as its makers prefer, the bike "rumbles with the echoes of Harleys past."

At a first glance, most onlookers took the Nostalgia – which was fresh from the

factory floor – to be either the real 1949 McCoy or a bespoke special that had been put together at huge expense by one of Hollywood's celebrity custom farms. Harley-Davidson's retro illusion was that good, yet only 2,700 examples of the limited-edition Nostalgia were ever built.

Even at $13,000 – just $3,100 less than the most lavish Glide – demand for these highly-desirable models far exceeded supply.

Second-hand "CowGlide" Nostalgias were soon changing hands at far more than list price. Mark up another masterpiece for Willie G. Davidson and his men.

■ BELOW *They say that nostalgia isn't what it used to be. No, in this case it's much better.*

FLSTF FAT BOY, 2000

The irreverently-named Fat Boy has held pride of place in Milwaukee's custom line-up since its debut in 1990. The FLSTF could claim to be the coolest of all the Retro-Techs, with its 16in (406mm) solid-disc wheels, elegant lines and bold but understated paint. For the year 2000, Fatso and its fellow Softails got the biggest shake-up since the line began back in 1984, with only a handful of parts retained from the old model. The new millennium marks the end of the noble 80-inch Evo engine and the adoption of the Twin Cam 88 across the entire heavyweight range.

This is no ordinary Twin Cam, though. Designated the 88B, the engine was developed in parallel with the "stock" 88 and uses essentially the same top ends, including the same 88.42cu in (1,449cc) displacement from identical bore and stroke dimensions. The bottom-end, however, features hardware never seen on any previous Harley: twin counter-rotating balance shafts. The eccentrically weighted shafts, tightly-packed inside the crankcases, rotate in

■ BELOW LEFT Only Harley could get away with such a derogatory title – and make it sell.

the opposite direction to the crankshaft to eliminate primary engine vibration.

This is necessary because the Softail rear suspension pretty much demands that the engine be mounted rigidly in the frame. As a consequence, the rubber mounting used to such good effect on other heavyweight models is not a practical option.

Since their inception, Softails have been marred by punishing vibration, especially at high revs, reducing their long-haul capability. Rideability has been dramatically improved with the 88B, offering true long-distance comfort. In keeping with this, fuel capacity was increased to 5 gallons (19 litres) and the tank is now one-piece, obviating the irritation of earlier twin fillers.

Although somewhat less powerful than Twin Cam Dynas and Glides, the 88B also offers more power and torque

SPECIFICATIONS	
Engine	air-cooled ohv V-twin
Capacity	88.42cu in (1,449cc)
Transmission	5-speed
Power	63bhp
Weight	666lbs (302kg)
Wheelbase	64.5in (1,637mm)
Top speed	106mph (170kph)

■ LEFT The first of the breed. Fender trim, backrest and saddlebags are non-standard.

■ RIGHT *The Fat Boy is actually no more of a fatso than other Softails, and its lines are cleaner, as these late-Evo versions clearly show.*

with substantially improved tractability. Maximum power is some 63bhp at 5,300rpm, with torque peaking at 78lb/ft (106Nm) at 3,500rpm. Uprated gearbox internals offer slicker, lighter gearshifts, easier neutral-finding and less transmission noise.

At the rear, a new drive belt is stronger and longer-lasting than before yet, at 1⅛in (28mm), almost ¼in (6mm) narrower in section. This permits a wider rear tyre, although – with less than 30 degrees of lean angle on offer – this is scarcely likely to promote scratching.

In addition, year 2000 Softails ride on an all-new frame, stiffer than before but fabricated from half as many parts – just 17 – as previous models. This is complemented by a redesigned swing arm which also contributes to a more stable ride. When it comes to hauling this 666lb (300kg) brute down from speed, even the brakes – long a Milwaukee blind-spot – have been substantially improved. Four piston callipers now grace both ends of the Fat Boy, and the disc rotors are more resistant to heat distortion. The effect is

■ LEFT *The very first FLSTF in metallic grey was widely considered the most handsome.*

■ BELOW *For year 2000 the Fat Boy benefited from the new 88B balance-shafted Twin Cam engine.*

improving braking power and a 20 per cent reduction in brake-lever effort.

This is a considerable catalogue of real improvements on any model, let alone one cherished more for its looks and style than its functional elan. The 2000 Fat Boy has received a few cosmetic touches – notably, restyled exhausts and rear mudguard – without losing any of its essential character, but Milwaukee has surely got it right by making it work far better, too.

Low Riders and Dynas

It's the Milwaukee way to create blend bikes which take on their own identity over the years, and these are a case in point. DynaGlides evolved from Low Riders, which evolved from SuperGlides, which in turn evolved when the factory first grafted a Sportster front end on to an ElectraGlide. The very first Low Rider, the FXS, appeared in 1977. At heart it was little more than a FXE SuperGlide, complete with 74-inch Shovelhead engine, yet within four years it had soared to become Harley-Davidson's best-selling non-Sportster model.

In 1980, the FXB Sturgis – essentially a Low Rider with belt drive and extended forks – was added to a growing FX series which now included SuperGlide, Low Rider, WideGlide and Fat Bob models. Despite their popularity, these were the last to receive the Evolution V2 engine, making do with Shovelheads until late in 1984.

Five-speed transmission was added model-by-model throughout 1985–6, but the most significant novelty was the appearance of a new chassis with the limited-edition FXDB Sturgis of 1991. Incorporating a magically effective, new two-point engine-mounting system, this has progressively replaced the old Low Rider frame on all FXD-series models. The family now comprises perhaps the most practical and versatile workhorses in the Harley-Davidson range.

FXRS-CONV LOW RIDER CONVERTIBLE, 1989–93

■ BELOW *The Convertible became the ultimate Harley all-rounder upon its launch for 1989.*

Characterized by their brutal, low lines, fat rear wheels and skinny front ends, Low Riders represented one of the core "families" of Milwaukee models from 1977 until the mid-1990s. Beginning with the 74-inch Shovelhead FXS in 1977, the range grew to include seminal spin-offs such as the FXEF Fat Bob and FXB Sturgis. Along the way, Low Rider capacity grew to 80cu in (1,338cc) for 1980 and adopted toothed-belt final drive for the FXSB of 1983. The first Evolution-engine Low Rider, the FXRS Custom Sport, appeared for the 1985 model year, gaining five-speed transmission one year later. By 1987, Harley's "broadest and most versatile range" included Standard, Custom and Sport Edition models, as well as sister models such as the quintessential Super-Glide and SportGlide.

Harley-Davidson literature was always keen to stress Low Riders' unrivalled "combination of style and comfort", and it was certainly true that the range always veered towards the practical end of the style scale: cruisers that are as adept on the open road as on the city streets.

"They're in their element anywhere there's pavement" was how the brochures put it. It was no idle boast.

This was never more apparent than with the Low Rider Convertible released for the 1989 season.

Although not exactly a convertible in the Cadillac sense, this model was as close as any two-wheeler needed to be. No longer did owners need to lash luggage wherever they could – this Convertible came complete with leather saddlebags. There was a large, wind-cheating Lexan screen, too. The real beauty of both was that they were detachable, and quickly. Riders setting out for the long haul could leave them on – or, in just a few moments, whip them off for a cruise downtown.

■ LEFT AND ABOVE LEFT *Easily detached screen and saddlebags made the FXRS equally at home in the western deserts as cruising city streets. The 1991 model (above) is en route from the Harley factory at York, Pennsylvania to San Francisco.*

SPECIFICATIONS

Engine	air-cooled ohv V-twin
Capacity	81.6cu in (1,340cc)
Transmission	5-speed
Power	69bhp
Weight	585lbs (265kg)
Wheelbase	64.7in (1,643mm)
Top speed	106mph (170kph)

■ BELOW *Successor to the FXRS-Conv is the DynaGlide Convertible, now with 88 Twin Cam power.*

As a touring alternative to Electra-Glide overkill, the Convertible was supreme. Its plush seat, standard sissy bar and highway pegs offered reasonable comfort (although the pillion pad was always something of a style-dictated joke), while the screen kept off the worst of road grime and weather. It handled tolerably well, too. The 1½in (39mm) front forks featured air-adjustment and anti-dive. For a heavyweight Harley, ground clearance was also good. Stopping was better than the Milwaukee norm – courtesy of twin hydraulic discs at the front and one at the rear.

The Low Rider look came largely from the choice of wheels: a 19in (483mm) front rim with a 100/90 tyre, compared to a 16in (406mm) rear hoop with a fat, 5⅛in- (130mm-) wide tread. Power came from the Evo 81.6cu in (1,340cc) mill. Although the rubber-mounting wasn't quite in the same league as modern Dyna

■ LEFT *Hot dry air and stinging dust make the screen essential in desert conditions.*

■ BELOW *Possibly not the most handsome chunk of Milwaukee iron, but very definitely one of the most practical. This is a 1992 example.*

models, it was pretty good. For five years until it gave way to the Dyna series at the end of 1993, the Low Rider Convertible was perhaps the most practical Harley-Davidson model. It was a neat adaptation of a well-

sorted design, so there were few improvements during the time. A 1⅜in (40mm) Keihin carb and improved clutch were introduced in 1990, and other minor details, but essentially the first one was as good as the last. In 1994, the FXRS gave way to another Convertible, the Dyna-series FXDS.

FXDB STURGIS, 1991

On the face of it, the "Mark II" Sturgis added little to the Low Rider family from which it sprang. Named after the annual North Dakota bike rally, the FXDB looked like little more than a midnight-black FXRS with modest changes to its rear shocks and oil tank. Indeed, the two models shared the same front end. The major attributes of the FXDB Sturgis were simplicity itself – just two hard-to-spot pieces of rubber – and with them, a motorcycle was transformed. The Sturgis was a limited-edition model – just over 1,500 were produced – but its impact lives on in every DynaGlide built since. The frame itself, an all-steel structure developed by advanced computer-aided design, is fabricated from a mixture of tubular and forged components with a large-diameter box-section backbone.

The engine isolation system differed from the existing Glide series and Low Rider mounts. These had used three location points with rubber-bonded

bolts, rather than the two more sophisticated composite blocks of the Sturgis. The result was startling. The big twin's effective rev range had been limited by low-speed shudders at the

SPECIFICATIONS	
Engine	air-cooled ohv V-twin
Capacity	81.6cu in (1,340cc)
Power	69bhp
Transmission	5-speed
Wheelbase	65.5in (1,665mm)
Weight	597lbs (271kg)
Top speed	106mph (170kph)

bottom end and intrusive vibes at the top. With the Sturgis, that all changed. One could now happily ride at engine speeds where other Hogs would rattle. Softails have the highest overall gearing of any model to reduce revs to comfortable vibration levels at cruising speeds. Fittingly, another Sturgis, the FXB, had been associated with two other momentous bits of rubber a decade earlier – the toothed rubber belts of its revolutionary primary and final drive.

■ ABOVE TOP AND CENTRE *Named after a major motorcycle rally, the Sturgis was a major leap forward in Harley affairs. It was to give rise to the stunningly successful Dyna-Glide series.*

■ LEFT *Stars and stripes had less to do with the Sturgis legacy than did two deceptively simple rubberized blocks.*

FXDWG DYNA WIDEGLIDE, 1993–PRESENT

By 1992, the Sturgis no longer existed, but it had spawned a growing DynaGlide family – first the Dyna Daytona, then the SuperGlide Dyna Custom. By 1993, the Dyna Low Rider was closer to the original but the WideGlide harked back to its namesake of the 1980s. Both, however, went one stage further than the Sturgis in the anti-vibration stakes, with revised "directionally-controlled" mounting blocks.

Harley's idea was "to combine the look of Low Riders of the late 1970s, with the handling and rubber-mounted ride of today", and it worked startlingly well. The 1993 DynaGlides were the smoothest Hogs yet, by a margin. Milwaukee's engineers had made a good bike better, even more than they had with the Sturgis. Without so much as laying a hand on the engine, the company had broadened the big V's effective powerband by a quantum amount – a bigger bonus than adding another ten horsepower.

Much of the rest, as is Harley's way, was in the hands of the blend-men and cosmetic engineers. There are "factory ape-hangers", a "tucked-in tail light", "air-foil directionals" and a wide front fork (hence the "WideGlide") with a 21in (533mm), wire-spoked front wheel, as well as a new, one-piece Fat Bob

■ RIGHT *An original 1993 WideGlide, so named because of the obvious width between the fork legs.*

■ BELOW *The badge might be fiery, but the vibrations were not, thanks to a revolutionary system of engine mounting.*

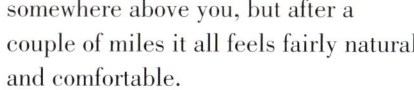

tank, which removed the need of having to fill up two separate fuel tanks each time you ran short on petrol (gas).

To ride the WideGlide is to marvel at the unprecedented smoothness of the experience – especially after you've grown accustomed to having only forward-mounted footpegs and controls. The ape-hanger handlebars tower somewhere above you, but after a couple of miles it all feels fairly natural and comfortable.

In that uncanny Harley-Davidson way, the steering is light with excellent low-speed balance.

Turns, however, reveal a lot about the WideGlide. Even by Harley-Davidson standards, ground clearance is poor. The stand scrapes on the left, the muffler on the right, both with sufficient force to pitch you off line.

But on the straight, wide highway, it's great to ride.

■ BELOW *For 1999 the new Twin Cam 88 engine was bestowed upon the redoubtable WideGlide.*

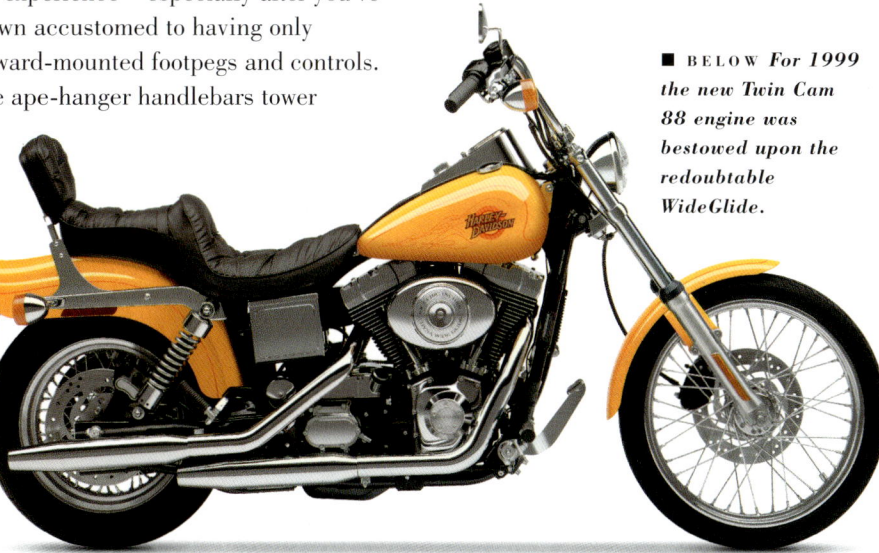

SPECIFICATIONS

Engine	air-cooled ohv V-twin
Capacity	81.6cu in (1,340cc)
Transmission	5-speed
Power	69bhp
Weight	598lbs (271kg)
Wheelbase	66.1in (1,680mm)
Top speed	106mph (170kph)

FXDX DYNA SUPERGLIDE SPORT, 1999–PRESENT

■ BELOW *With its understated lines, the FXDX is as stylish as previous Dynas.*

The FXDX Dyna SuperGlide Sport is much more than just the first model to be fitted with the new Twin Cam powerplant. True, the 88.42cu in (1,449cc) engine will attract the most fuss and gives the latest Dyna more get-up-and-go than any previous Milwaukee model, but the rest of the bike offers even more surprises – this is a Harley that stops and handles. For once, the "Sport" in the title means what it says.

Compared to the 80-inch Evo, the Dyna's blacked-out Twin Cam 88 engine runs a bigger 3⅞in (95.25mm) bore with a shortened 4in (101.6mm) stroke. Despite a ten per cent increase in capacity, the result is a powerplant that spins up faster yet with less vibration and a higher rev ceiling of 5,500rpm. The high-pressure, die-cast aluminium crankcases possess a strengthened vertical rear face across which four high-tensile bolts connect the engine to the five-speed transmission. The resulting structure is more rigid than before, reducing stress on the inner

primary drive and reducing overall vibration levels. The crankcases themselves are lighter and stronger due to design changes in high-stress areas, redesigned tappet guides and the relocation of the oil pump. Chain cam drive, in place of the previous straight-

cut gears, is not only cheaper to produce but also one of several measures aimed at reducing mechanical noise in the face of increasing environmental concerns. Great effort has also been put into improving even the Evo's record of durability, with the all-new pressed-up

■ ABOVE *The FXDX was the first Harley to be fitted with the Twin Cam powerplant, the chain drive to which can be seen here.*

■ LEFT *The Dyna can be adjusted to suit any riding style.*

■ RIGHT *Gliding along on the open road.*

crankshaft featuring new forged flywheels, beefier connecting rods and an uprated crank pin – all of which should easily withstand the Twin Cam's prodigious torque – over 78lb/ft (106Nm) at a mere 2,900rpm. O-rings replace the Evo's cylinder base gaskets, allowing a sturdier and more oil-tight joint between the crankcase and

cylinders, as well as enhancing temperature tolerance and reducing bore distortion. Of course, Harley's trademark air-cooling is retained, but a 50 per cent increase in fin area on the cylinders and cylinder heads improves its effect.

If the 88's eager power makes it a real joy to ride, the chassis is at least as rewarding. The frame is substantially similar to previous Evo-engined Dynas, with the same highly effective rubber mounting system insulating rider and passenger from vibration. By the standards of many Harley-Davidson heavyweights, the Dyna runs relatively little trail at just over 4in (104mm) and thus turns more eagerly, but it's the suspension that makes the difference – as big a departure as

was the DuoGlide's more than four decades earlier. Both the forks and the Japanese Showa rear shock absorbers now feature full adjustment of preload, rebound and compression damping. Whatever type of riding you have in mind, the Dyna can be adjusted to suit.

Winding up the damping at both ends won't turn the 614lb (279kg) FXDX into a sports bike, but it certainly allows it to corner like no previous big Hog. It still wallows to a degree through fast, bumpy turns, but handles with reassuring precision even at three-figure speeds. Ground clearance is also better. When the time comes to slow down, the latest Dyna is up to the challenge, thanks to a trio of four-piston Hayes calipers biting hard on 11½in (292mm) discs.

Cosmetically, the newcomer sports the same understated lines as previous Dynas, with flat, dirt track style handlebars, a low-line saddle, acres of moody black and a relatively restrained sprinkling of chrome.

Maybe that's just how it should be, for perhaps more than any other Milwaukee musclebike, this is the one that least needs to shout about its virtues.

SPECIFICATIONS

Engine	air-cooled ohv V-twin
Capacity	88.42cu in (1,449cc)
Transmission	5-speed
Power	86bhp
Weight	614lbs (279kg)
Wheelbase	64in (1,623mm)
Top speed	115mph (185kph)

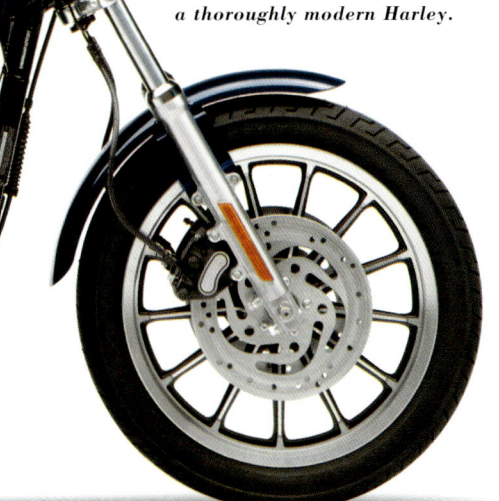

■ LEFT *The Twin Cam FXDX – a thoroughly modern Harley.*

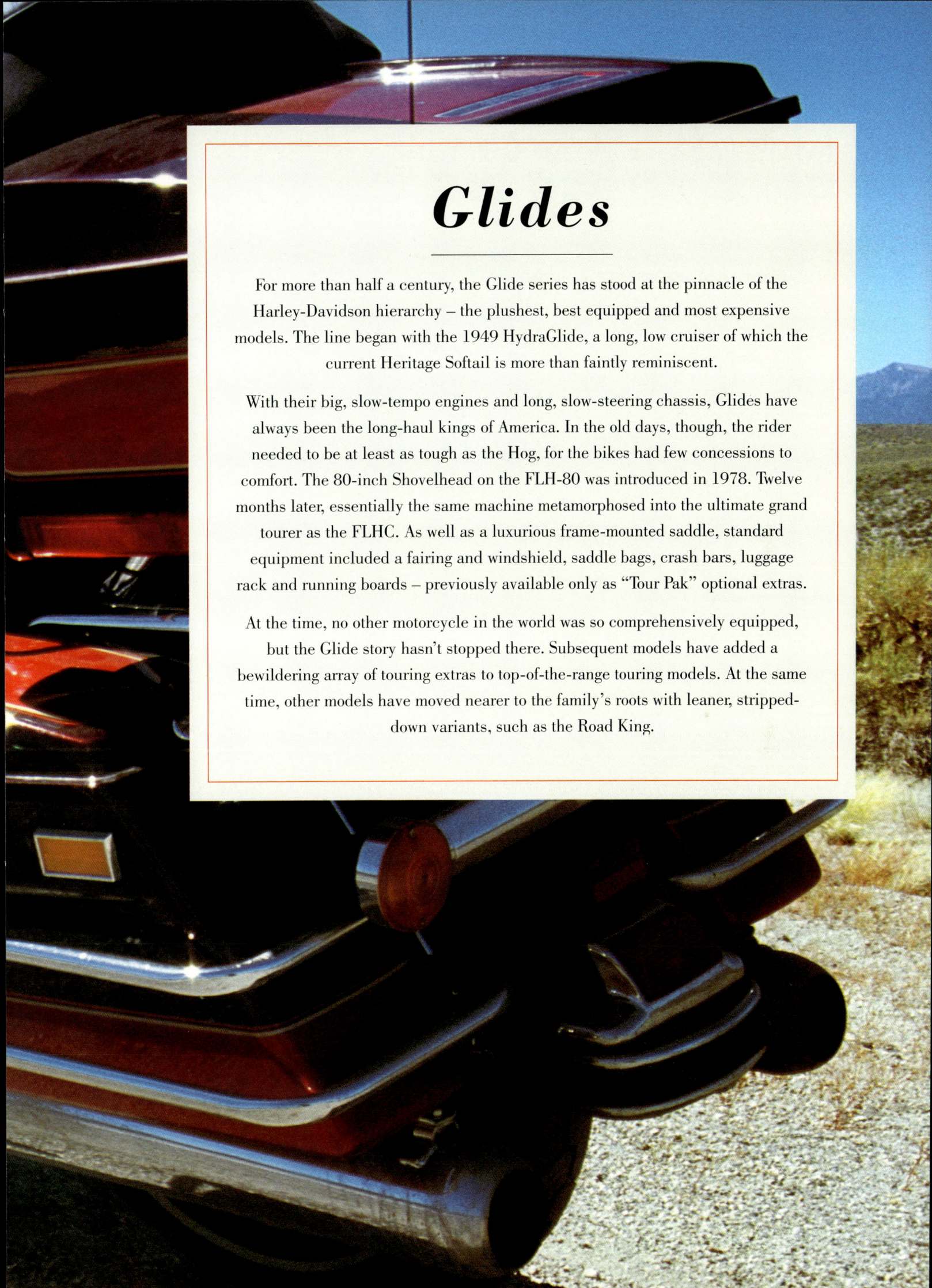

Glides

For more than half a century, the Glide series has stood at the pinnacle of the Harley-Davidson hierarchy – the plushest, best equipped and most expensive models. The line began with the 1949 HydraGlide, a long, low cruiser of which the current Heritage Softail is more than faintly reminiscent.

With their big, slow-tempo engines and long, slow-steering chassis, Glides have always been the long-haul kings of America. In the old days, though, the rider needed to be at least as tough as the Hog, for the bikes had few concessions to comfort. The 80-inch Shovelhead on the FLH-80 was introduced in 1978. Twelve months later, essentially the same machine metamorphosed into the ultimate grand tourer as the FLHC. As well as a luxurious frame-mounted saddle, standard equipment included a fairing and windshield, saddle bags, crash bars, luggage rack and running boards – previously available only as "Tour Pak" optional extras.

At the time, no other motorcycle in the world was so comprehensively equipped, but the Glide story hasn't stopped there. Subsequent models have added a bewildering array of touring extras to top-of-the-range touring models. At the same time, other models have moved nearer to the family's roots with leaner, stripped-down variants, such as the Road King.

FLTCU TourGlide Ultra, 1989–96

After the ElectraGlide, Sportster and SuperGlide, the TourGlide was one of the most enduring packages in the entire Milwaukee line up. The concept – the most "loaded" machine Harley-Davidson engineers could imagine – began with the basic FLT TourGlide of 1980. At the time, the TourGlide offered the nearest thing you could buy to a two-wheeled limousine. Small refinements to the already profoundly refined machine followed year-on-year, not to mention the adoption of belt final drive and Evo V2 power in 1984. The basic concept was still fine, but as the decade was drawing to a close, an even more luxurious carriage was needed. It arrived in 1989 with the awesome TourGlide Ultra Classic, 81.6cu in (1,340cc) of imposing, luxurious brawn. As well as obvious features, such as new fairing "lowers" to protect the rider, a welter of electronics graced the big Glide. From the saddle, the rider now had control of

a mouth-watering array of on-board refinement. At the rider's fingertips, there was now electronic cruise control, CB radio and a sophisticated stereo hi-fi

system. Even the pillion was provided with separate speakers and a built-in intercom allowed rider and passenger to chew the fat. A cigarette lighter was

■ ABOVE *A 1991 TourGlide in its element, easing across the high desert plateau of Utah, in the south-western United States.*

■ LEFT *The last of a majestic line, a fuel-injected FLTCUI Ultra Classic TourGlide from the 1996 model year.*

■ **LEFT** *Copious luggage capacity and excellent rider protection are clear from this image of a TourGlide crossing Nevada's wide-open spaces.*

SPECIFICATIONS	
Engine	air-cooled ohv V-twin
Capacity	81.6cu in (1,340cc)
Transmission	5-speed
Power	69bhp
Weight	765lbs (347kg)
Wheelbase	63in (1,600mm)
Top speed	105mph (169kph)

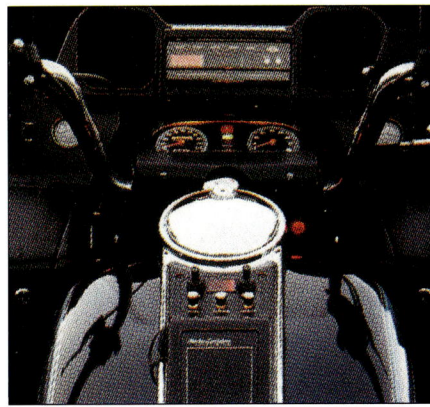

■ **ABOVE** *The rider's cockpit perspective of the Ultra Classic TourGlide.*

■ **BELOW** *The majestic spirit of the Glides lives on in this 1992 TourGlide.*

In 1990, I rode a TourGlide from the Harley-Davidson factory in York, Pennsylvania, to San Francisco, California, on America's west coast. Along the way, the big Glide had thumped up endless gradients to more than 11,000ft (3,300m), rumbled across baking deserts for hour after hour, splashed through thunderstorms and scarcely missed a beat. It carried me and everything I needed for 4,000 miles (6,500km), and everyone I met smiled in appreciation. For this sort of experience – traversing the vast emptiness of the United States – no other motorcycle comes anywhere close to it. It was almost as though the TourGlide evolved there – which, come to think of it, it did.

The TourGlide story has ended – for the time being, at least. After 16 years as the long-haul king of America's open roads, the name was dropped from the Harley line-up after the fuel-injected FLTCUI model of 1996. However, its spirit still lives on in the extravagantly equipped Ultra Classic ElectraGlides.

standard and even the self-cancelling indicators were microprocessor-controlled. To cope with this plethora of added electrical demands, a new high-output 32-amp alternator was also fitted.

Overkill? Perhaps, but profoundly practical too. The panniers and capacious "Tour-Pak" top-box easily swallowed two weeks' luggage. The plush, upholstered saddle was good for long, long days on the road, while the screen kept dust and dry desert winds at bay. True, a sound system as good as the one at home isn't strictly necessary on a motorcycle, but who can resist cruising enchanted landscapes to a favourite blues tune, all to a backbeat of a thundering Milwaukee twin?

FLHR ElectraGlide Road King, 1994–Present

As standard equipment became even more comprehensive at the top of the ElectraGlide range, there came a demand for a model more like the stripped-down FLs of the 1960s. Harley-Davidson's response was the FLHS Sport of 1987 – a real lightweight at "only" 690lbs (313kg). Today's handsome FLHR Road King is in much the same mould.

Launched for the 1994 season, the Road King was an attempt to bridge the gap between Milwaukee's custom and touring models. Although in essence a full-on ElectraGlide minus the fairing, with a "retro" chromed headlight and tank-mounted speedometer, its long, low silhouette belied its super-heavyweight roots. Here was a machine that could hit the highway with the same authority as any other Glide – once the detachable windscreen was installed. As well as the QD windshield (an idea borrowed from the Low Rider Convertible), the panniers and pillion perch were also easily removed, changing the machine's profile and character in the wink of an eye. Thus

■ ABOVE *Cleaner, lower lines distinguish this king of the road from other heavyweight FLs.*

■ BELOW *Adding a few of Milwaukee's many accessories can undermine the effect.*

stripped, the King had all the languid grace of a custom cruiser.

To most eyes this is the best looking of all the Glides, the normally ponderous lines replaced by a machine which, if not exactly svelte, has a certain grace. Where fully-loaded FLs tend to obesity, the Road King has style. It's a Harley-Davidson for those who want their heavyweight cake in custom clothes.

Equally, its touring roots make the King an eminently practical custom bike. Six hours in the saddle is hard work on any Softail but a Glide can comfortably knock that off – and more.

SPECIFICATIONS

Engine	air-cooled ohv V-twin
Capacity	81.6cu in (1,340cc)
Transmission	5-speed
Power	69bhp
Weight	692lbs (314kg)
Wheelbase	62.7in (1,590mm)
Top speed	100mph (161kph)

■ **LEFT AND BELOW** *The "Road King" badge and overall detailing is pure 1960s, although the other chromework (below) is aftermarket kit.*

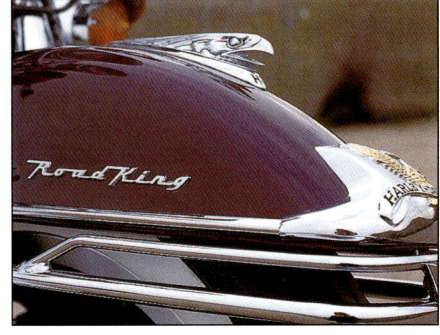

The rubber-mounted Evo engine keeps vibration at bay but lets that evocative rumble pour through. Parked anywhere it looks good; on the open road, it works.

The first fuel-injected Road King, the FLHRI came in 1996, although carburetted versions continued to be produced in parallel. The ESPFI (Electronic Sequential Port Fuel Injection) system is based on a similar Italian Magneti Marelli design to that of Ducati V-twins, although in this case the emphasis is on user-friendliness rather than sheer power. Though some owners may prefer the reassuring simplicity of a stock single carb poking out of the right-hand side, the new fuel-injection system is a major bonus. As well as improving emissions, it offers slightly higher torque

(83lb/ft rather than 79lb0/ft) and much better driveability, particularly at high altitude. The fuel system was improved across the Injection range for 1997.

High-tech is largely absent elsewhere, except of course for Harley-Davidson's trademark belt final drive. Suspension is adjustable only for air pressure in the twin rear shock absorbers. Both wheels are cast light alloy, 16in (406mm) in diameter, wearing characteristically fat Glide rubber.

Twin hydraulic disc brakes grace the front, with a single disc at the rear. All three of these brakes have a lot of work to do on a machine that scales 692lbs (314kg), but these days, Harley-Davidson

stoppers work fairly well. Like most of the Glide family, the Road King's top speed is maybe a shade over 100mph (161kph), although screaming the big twin that hard is a futile pursuit.

The Road King is happiest when it is ambling along at a disdainful 75mph (120kph); if you travel at much above 85mph (140kph), a disconcerting weave has sometimes been known to intrude.

To be king of the road the Milwaukee way, you don't need to be the fastest – just the coolest.

■ **LEFT** *A 1996 Road King – or should that be FLHR-Convertible? Both the windshield and pillion seat are quickly detachable.*

FLHTCU-I ULTRA CLASSIC ELECTRAGLIDE, 1997–PRESENT

For a supposedly conservative model from a fairly cautious company, the top ElectraGlide has undergone a relentless battery of changes during the past few years. Fuel injection (ESPFI) first hit the family on the FLHTC Thirtieth Anniversary in 1995, before becoming standard on Road King and top-of-the-range ElectraGlides for the following model year. Then, scarcely had 1997 brought a new frame with lower saddle height (27in/685mm) and many other detail changes, than Harley-Davidson's first new engine for 15 years graced the good old ElectraGlide.

The Twin Cam 88 is not only "glittering with chrome" but gives the massive ElectraGlide a welcome boost to more than 80bhp, with a prodigious peak torque of 86lb/ft (117Nm). With a wider spread of torque and the driveability that only fuel injection brings, the big Glide's legendary ability to gobble up countless miles is

■ ABOVE *With its luxuriously cushioned seat, riding the Ultra Classic is a dream.*

■ BELOW *An Evo-engined predecessor to the full-on Ultra Classic 88. But who'd want his electricity bill?*

improved. Now it shrugs off gradients and altitude with even greater ease than before. Everything about the big Glide, from its fat tyres and sofa-like saddle to lazy, laid-back steering geometry, marks it out as the grandest of open-road tourers.

Scaling a thundering 776lbs (352kg) without so much as a drop of fuel in the tank, this is the heaviest Hog of them all. Most of that weight is good, solid Milwaukee metal, but much of the rest aims to pamper the rider like no other bike known to humanity. The amply

SPECIFICATIONS	
Engine	air-cooled ohv V-twin
Capacity	88.42cu in (1,449cc)
Transmission	5-speed
Power	80bhp
Weight	776lbs (352kg)
Wheelbase	63in (1,600mm)
Top speed	105mph (169kph)

■ RIGHT *With plenty of room to store luggage, this is the ultimate long-haul Hog.*

padded seat is huge and welcoming, while the adjustable footboards give room to move and relax. Harley's neat method of rubber mounting the engine in the steel square-backbone frame ensures that engine vibration is enough to say "Harley" but not so that it will intrude. Meanwhile the panniers, fairing pockets and copious, carpet-lined "King Tour-Pak" top box simply swallow up luggage.

Harley-Davidson describes its top model as "fully loaded" and you'd better believe it. Depending on the market, it comes with passing and running lamps, more instruments than a Boeing and even a cigarette lighter. There's a voice-activated intercom, CB radio and electronic cruise control complete with "Resume" and "Accelerate" modes. The 40-watts-per-channel AM/FM cassette radio contains weatherband, four speakers, separate passenger controls and dual antenna, all controlled

from a myriad of switches on the left handlebar and able to respond automatically to ambient noise levels.

If any Harley-Davidson is as much fantasy as motorcycle, this top ElectraGlide takes the dream to the next level. Imagine cruising over Arizona's high plateaux, the warm desert wind tugging at your sleeves and caressing your designer sunglasses. Slip in your favourite blues cassette or tune in to a passing country music station, and the

Glide will transport you to Hog heaven. Come service time, it can even talk to Harley-Davidson mechanics as well, since the engine management system contains full diagnostic capability – and that's only part of the story.

Some bikers mock the ElectraGlide as a two-wheeled Cadillac de Ville. Certainly, it's as far from a sports bike as it is possible for a motorcycle to get.

Absurd, to some.

Over-the-top, probably.

But glorious – definitely yes.

■ LEFT *The biggest, most expensive and most magnificent model in the Harley-Davidson range, the mighty fuel-injected ElectraGlide Ultra Classic.*

FLHRCI ROAD KING CLASSIC, 2000

■ **BELOW** *The aristocratic Road King Classic, a new breed of style machine.*

The Classic version of the Road King takes up where the standard model left off. In terms of straight specification, there is little to set the two models apart. Yet the Classic, as the name suggests, is a different sort of hybrid: a full-on tourer which is also a custom machine.

With laced (spoked) wheels and fat whitewall tyres, chrome-fringed saddlebags and swept-back lines, the King Classic is almost as svelte as the ElectraGlide is gross – or, as Harley puts it, "has enough traditional styling to drop jaws throughout the continent". Indeed, throughout any continent.

So, for a tourer, the Classic screams "style". As well as those wheels and tyres, it's in the custom metal emblems on the tank, fender tips and seat. It's in that bold trademark , chromed headlamp and twin 35-watt passing lights. It's in the chrome dual mufflers and stainless-steel "Buffalo" handlebars and – new for 2000 – in classic two-tone paint.

As with all year 2000 big-twin models, power comes from the Twin Cam 88 engine first unveiled the previous year. The 88.42cu in (1,449cc) ohv V-twin features electronic fuel injection via 1½in (38mm) inlet stacks – and, not least, an attention-grabbing chrome-and-black engine finish. Other than its

SPECIFICATIONS	
Engine	air-cooled ohv V-twin
Capacity	88.42cu in (1,449cc)
Transmission	5-speed
Power	80bhp
Weight	710lb (322kg)
Wheelbase	63⅓in (1,612mm)
Top speed	110mph (177kph)

long-legged lump, the King's touring credentials lie with its leather saddlebags (with rigid inserts to prevent their going out of shape), well-upholstered seat, Lexan windshield (quickly detachable for town riding) and 5-gallon (19-litre) fuel tank. In addition, both rider and pillion foot-boards can be adjusted to the right height.

Once upon a time, Milwaukee might have been content with leaving it at that, but not any more. In recent times, it has actively sought greater user-friendliness and better performance on all fronts. So, in common with its fellow heavyweights (except the Springer Softail), the feeble old brakes give way to four-pot calipers

(heavy-weights have two at the front), squeezing uprated friction pads on to much-improved 11½in (292mm) rotors. Both braking power and feel are improved as a result, while lever effort is reduced substantially.

There are new wheel bearings, maintenance-free for 100,000 miles (160,000km). The same goes for the new sealed, long-life, 28Ah battery.

The King Classic is built as vast as only Harley-Davidson knows how, scaling over 700lbs (320kg) without so much as a drop of fuel in its Fat Bob tank. Tying the plot together is a massive mild-steel frame with heavyweight box-section spine and twin tubular cradles.

Suspension at both ends is air-adjustable, although wheel travel is less than generous.

The HydraGlide-style forks offer 4.6in (117mm) of movement while the twin rear shock absorbers afford (3in) 76mm. The King Classic will change direction in its own good time, and has 6.1in (155mm) of trail and a gargantuan wheelbase of 63⅓in (1,612mm). Which is precisely the point: where's the dignity in rushing?

■ ABOVE *An Evo-engined 1997 Heritage Springer Softail. The latest version benefits enormously from the smoothness of the Twin Cam 88B powerplant.*

Buell

The name might be unfamiliar and Buell may not have the length of pedigree of the Harley-Davidson company, but they do have deep and fertile roots. The breed arose from the efforts of former racer Erik Buell, who began creating his idiosyncratic line of racing specials in 1983. The first of these, the RW750, had a four-cylinder 750cc two-stroke engine and was capable of around 180mph (290kph) – very un-Harley fare. When this was outlawed by a change in racing regulations, Buell began his first Harley-engined project, the RR1000.

A total of 50 of these XR1000-engined machines were produced during 1987–8, before the focus switched to the new 1,200cc Evolution powerplant and the RR1200 model. Tuned versions of the same 1200 Sportster engine have powered all Buell models since. All bore tribute to Buell's innovative approach to design, particularly with respect to their lightweight monoshock chassis with advanced suspension and braking components.

It is precisely these attributes that now differentiate Buell Harleys from the more traditional Harley-Davidson models. Buell does not build cruisers or customs – or tourers in the heavyweight Milwaukee sense. Buells are sports bikes, sports tourers or "in your face" streetfighter machines. They still have Harley-Davidson soul and presence, but they have added muscle and attitude, too.

M2 Cyclone & S3 Thunderbolt

■ M2 CYCLONE

"It came from a motorcyclist's soul, not from a product planning committee," is the Buell promotional slogan, and it fits the streetfighting Cyclone to a "T". The base model of the East Troy range when launched in late 1996, the Cyclone is propelled by a tuned 1,200cc Sportster mill. Claimed peak power is a shuddering 86bhp – more than even the new Twin Cam 88. A wickedly broad torque band peaks at 79lb/ft (107Nm) at 5,400rpm.

The Cyclone runs on slightly less exotic chassis components than its siblings, notably conventional Showa teles rather than upside-down forks. All Buell models employ a single White Power rear unit located under the engine. Bodywork is kept to a minimum, showing the chrome-molybdenum steel perimeter frame off to maximum effect. The big twin engine is located using Buell's patented "Uniplanar" mountings, with tie-rods to reduce the effects of vibration. Final drive is via a reinforced toothed-belt similar to the mainstream Harley range. Although

■ RIGHT *The Cyclone has style, speed and attitude. What more could you want?*

■ BELOW *Sleek yet brutal – the Buell Thunderbolt.*

bestowed with only a single front disc, this offers an enormous friction area swept by a huge six-piston caliper. Both wheels are cast aluminium and of lightweight, three-spoke design. With a frame weighing a mere 26lbs (12kg), the Cyclone is fully 77lbs (35kg) lighter and more than 10bhp stronger than a 1200S Sportster. With these impressive numbers and this quality of chassis kit, the Cyclone and its kin handle and stop like no conventional Harley. Soul and speed are not mutually exclusive.

■ S3 THUNDERBOLT

The Thunderbolt, launched for 1997, was based around a chassis assembly similar to the then top-of-the-range S1

Lightning, mated to the Cyclone's 86bhp carburetted big twin engine. The race-bred chassis features fully-adjustable inverted White Power forks and under-slung rear suspension unit, with similar wheels and brakes to the Cyclone's. The Sportster-derived engine produces a claimed 86bhp at a giddy 6,000rpm and 79lb/ft (107Nm) of torque. The motor enjoys the same Uniplanar anti-vibration mountings as other Buell models, allowing plenty of gutsy rumble to reach the rider but damping out more destructive vibes. Visually, the T-bolt is distinguished by its swooping rear bodywork and aerodynamic fairing. Buell produces a sports-touring version, the S3T, with legshields and panniers.

SPECIFICATIONS: CYCLONE (THUNDERBOLT)	
Engine	ohv 45 degree V-twin
Capacity	1,203cc
Transmission	5-speed, toothed-belt final drive
Power	86bhp
Weight	434lbs/197kg (450lbs/204kg)
Wheelbase	55½in/1,410mm
Top speed	126mph/203kph (133mph/214kph)

BUELL HISTORY

Following the modest success of the Sportster-powered RR1200 (of which 65 were built), 1989 marked the debut of the first two-seater Buell, the RS1200 from which the single-seat RSS1200 evolved two years later. By this time, inverted telescopic forks and six-piston disc-brake calipers had become the norm for a marque which was rapidly grabbing the attention of the motorcycle community. By the end of 1992, the company had built a total of 442 machines and brought its founder a solid reputation for engineering and design.

In February 1993, Buell became part of the Harley-Davidson empire when Milwaukee bought a 49 per cent stake in the company. The merger gave Buell access to development funds and Harley-Davidson expertise while offering Harley a direct avenue into Buell's creative engineering. Buell was in fact collaborating with Harley on design as early as the late 1970s when he contributed to the original belt-drive Sturgis project.

■ LEFT *A rare Buell RS1200 from around 1989. Its heritage is evident.*

■ BELOW LEFT *The Buell assembly line in East Troy, an hour from Milwaukee, shown before Harley bought in.*

■ BELOW *The Buell's raw lines and radical engineering are abundantly clear with body-work removed.*

Buells are now built at East Troy, Wisconsin, using engines made at the "small powertrains" plant on Milwaukee's Capitol Drive. Now marketed in parallel with mainstream Harley-Davidson machines, the current generation of Cyclone, Thunderbolt and Lightning Buell models was first launched in the United States in 1994.

BUELL X1 LIGHTNING, 1999

Sharing a name with a 3,000mph (5000kph) jet plane, the X1 Lightning replaced the S-series Lightning when launched for 1999. This is a mean and purposeful "Streetfighter" from the makers of "Harleys with attitude".

The X1 is a truly credible sports machine. It bristles with character, and its power and handling are vastly improved compared to more traditional Milwaukee fare. At the X1's heart is a reworked "Thunderstorm"

SPECIFICATIONS

Engine	ohv 45 degree V-twin with EFI
Capacity	1,203cc
Transmission	5-speed, toothed-belt final drive
Power	95bhp (see main text)
Weight	439lbs (199kg)
Wheelbase	55½in (1,410mm)
Top speed	135mph (217kph)

version of the familiar 1,203cc Sportster engine with higher compression pistons, larger valves and ports re-profiled for improved gas flow. Lighter flywheels improve engine response and at the same time quicken the Sportster's normally leisurely gearchange.

Best of all is the X1's new and ultra-sophisticated Dynamic Digital fuel injection. The system uses state-of-the-art computer control to ensure that the big V-twin delivers its best under all conditions, virtually eliminating flat-spots, improving fuel economy and

cleaning up exhaust emissions. The result is one of the sharpest Harley-Davidson's ever built – and perhaps the most powerful.

According to independent dyno tests, peak power is 85bhp at 5,300rpm – more than any other stock Harley; the X1's torque is even more impressive:

■ ABOVE *The X1 Lightning: a real mean street-fighting machine.*

■ LEFT *With its minimalist seat design, this is a far cry from the ElectraGlide.*

Handling, too, is top notch. With its short, nimble wheelbase and only 3½in (89mm) of trail, the X1 turns quickly by Harley standards, inviting riders to dive hard into turns. Stability, too, is surprisingly good, allowing the machine to be ridden with confidence under almost any circumstances. Its minimalist seat and overall ergonomics may fall a long way short of ElectraGlide territory, but the sort of owners the X1 is aimed at will not mind that.

This impressive package is cloaked in the sort of eye-catching yet understated muscular styling for which the East Troy streetfighting machines have become renowned.

With a Buell, what you see is what you get – and you get the best Buell yet with the X1 Lightning.

92lb/ft (125Nm) at just 3,300rpm, guaranteeing a broad range of solid, usable power (Buell actually claims 95bhp and 85lb/ft (115Nm).

With this engine there is almost no such thing as being in the wrong gear: simply wind open the throttle and the big twin will deliver the goods at almost any rpm. Top speed is around 136mph (220kph), although this can vary as some markets receive models with raised gearing to help meet local noise limits.

Pinning all of this to the road is a rugged tubular steel trellis chassis, with new Japanese Showa suspension components at both ends. At the front are sturdy inverted forks which are adjustable for pre-load, compression and rebound damping.

The monoshock rear end offers built-in rising rate, plus pre-load and two-way damping tuning. The stainless-steel exhaust is tucked tight in, providing maximum room and comfort for one- or two-up riding and giving the best cornering ground clearance of any Milwaukee roadster, allowing the X1 to exploit to the full its Dunlop rubber. Although the Lightning boasts only a single front disc, braking is excellent as well, with a brawny 13.4in (340mm) rotor grabbed by a huge, six-piston "Performance Machine" caliper. A simple single-piston caliper and 9in (230mm) disc adorn the rear.

■ LEFT *Burnouts are easy thanks to tuned 1,200cc Sportster power.*

■ BELOW *Truly awesome: the Buell X1 Lightning.*

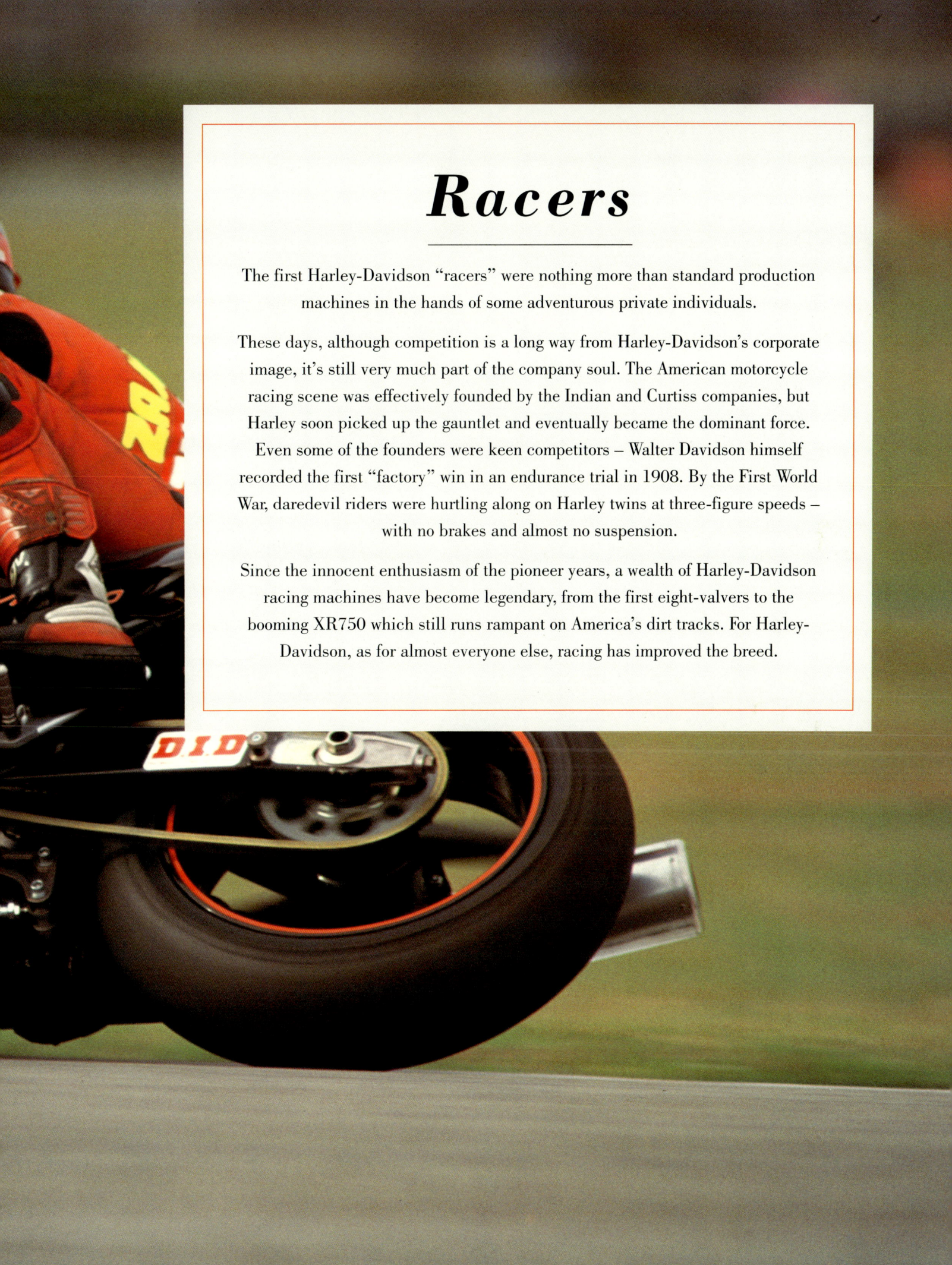

Racers

The first Harley-Davidson "racers" were nothing more than standard production machines in the hands of some adventurous private individuals.

These days, although competition is a long way from Harley-Davidson's corporate image, it's still very much part of the company soul. The American motorcycle racing scene was effectively founded by the Indian and Curtiss companies, but Harley soon picked up the gauntlet and eventually became the dominant force. Even some of the founders were keen competitors – Walter Davidson himself recorded the first "factory" win in an endurance trial in 1908. By the First World War, daredevil riders were hurtling along on Harley twins at three-figure speeds – with no brakes and almost no suspension.

Since the innocent enthusiasm of the pioneer years, a wealth of Harley-Davidson racing machines have become legendary, from the first eight-valvers to the booming XR750 which still runs rampant on America's dirt tracks. For Harley-Davidson, as for almost everyone else, racing has improved the breed.

EARLY RACERS

■ EIGHT-VALVE, TWO-CAM

Although a special "7-E" competition version of Harley-Davidson's first V-twin was built for selected customers as early as 1910, the first model created specifically for racing was the eight-valve twin which appeared in 1916. The multi-valve layout had already been amply proven by the exploits of Indian's similar engine, already the winner of the Isle of Man TT.

Displacing 61cu in (999cc), the Harley-Davidson eight-valve was the device on which the Harley Wrecking Crew began their domination of the American racing scene.

Private individuals were less fortunate, since the machine's price – $1,500 – was deliberately inflated to ensure that it could only fall into serious hands.

A 65cu in (1,065cc) twin-cam racer followed. Like the eight-valve model, the Two-Cam had inlet-over-exhaust valve layout, no brakes and direct drive by chain to the rear wheel (although some examples may have used three-speed transmissions). Once started – no easy task due to the use of very high

■ LEFT *A handsome 74-inch J-series racer dating from 1924. Note the total lack of any sort of brakes.*

■ LEFT *A 1924 74-inch F-head racer. Exhaust silencing was not a prime concern.*

■ BELOW *Another F-head, a 1920 board racer ridden by Dewey Sims. The plunger on the left side of the tank feeds engine oil.*

compression ratios – these monsters were capable of well over 100mph (160kph). To promote its wares overseas, Harley-Davidson freighted its top racing machines all over the world. In Britain, both Freddie Dixon and D.H. Davidson took the Two-Cam to numerous records at the famed banked Brooklands circuit in Surrey. In September 1923, at Arpajon in France, Dixon took the same machine to a world-record speed of 106.5mph (171.4kph).

■ OHV TWINS

During the mid-1920s, the F-head Two-Cam was the mainstay of Harley-Davidson's factory twin-cylinder racing efforts, but they were seriously hampered when the AMA introduced the new "Class C" racing formula. This was dispute as to whether they were actually created in Harley's competition shop or by a local dealer, Bill Knuth, with the factory's knowledge and support.

In either case, this was an interim measure, because twelve months later a 45-inch factory racer, the DAH, first appeared.

Unlike the Two-Cam-based machines, the DAH was substantially a new engine from the ground up, although it still depended on cylinder heads derived from the Peashooter's.

Displacing 45.44cu in (744cc), the DAH retained the 88.9mm stroke of the JD, but with a bore reduced to 70.6mm.

The DAH was dominant for a while, but Knuth came back with a four-cam hybrid reputed to produce fully 45 horsepower, which continued to give the official factory machines a run for their money. There are even records of a 61-inch ohv racing twin, designated FAR, being built for export.

It is highly likely that, in some measure or other, these exotic racing models were to inspire the later Knucklehead ohv twin. What is for certain is the profound influence that they had on the racing world at large.

for production-based 45cu in (750cc) machines, of which at least 25 had to be built. Overnight, the old Class A and Class B factory specials were relegated to the sidelines in much of American racing – especially in the buoyant "slant-shooting" (hill-climbing) scene.

At the time, Milwaukee produced no eligible machine, but by 1926 it did have the remarkably fast 21-inch ohv Peashooter single, and any darn fool could see that two times 21 wasn't far from 45. It wasn't long before someone investigated the possibility of grafting Peashooter heads on to existing V-twin bottom ends.

The first such ohv Harley-Davidson twin was probably a machine dubbed "Home Brew", ridden with some success by Oscar Lenz in 1927. A similar device, also based on a 61-inch bottom end, was built by Ralph Moore of Indianapolis.

By 1928, Harley-Davidson had given in to popular demand and released "roadster" versions of its Two-Cam racing twins, the 61-inch JH and 74-inch JDH and it wasn't long before Juneau Avenue followed the example of creative privateers with a number of factory specials featuring ohv Peashooter top ends grafted on to JD Two-Cam crankcases.

These first hit the tracks in 1928 at Fond du Lac, just a few miles north of Milwaukee. However, there is some

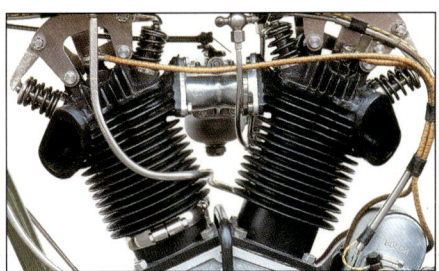

■ ABOVE *Four overhead valves per cylinder can clearly be seen in this view of the same 1923 eight-valver. Note the single carburettor between the cylinders.*

■ BELOW *Compared to the exotic factory eight-valvers, F-head board racers such as this were relatively low-tech, but still capable of frightening speeds.*

PEASHOOTER, 1929

As legendary in its way as was the exotic Two-Cam, the Peashooter began life as a standard roadster model. The Peashooter was based on the overhead-valve Model AA magneto version of the 21.1cu in (346cc) single produced from 1926 to 1935, which proved itself more than amenable to race tuning. Perhaps this was not altogether surprising, as the cylinder head – the most crucial performance element in any four-stroke engine – was designed by the great Harry Ricardo, the British engineering genius. Only a few years earlier, Ricardo had created Triumph's first four-valve motor, the Model R. Sir Harry, as he was later to become, practically invented the art of petrol- (gas-) flowing and, during

■ LEFT *The cylinder head of the Peashooter was designed by Harry Ricardo, a British engineer.*

■ BELOW *This single became a legend on the race tracks of the United States.*

SPECIFICATIONS	
Engine	ohv single
Capacity	21.1cu in (346cc)
Transmission	1- or 3-speed
Weight	290lbs (132kg)
Wheelbase	55in (1,400mm)
Top Speed	over 80mph (128kph)

the course of developing the concept of octane ratings for fuel, gained an unparalleled understanding of the combustion process.

Central to the Peashooter's success were two things. One was the engine's hemispherical "squish" heads, in which the outer portion of the piston crown almost touches the cylinder head as it rises up the bore. This in turn creates a fierce turbulence, promoting fuel/air mixing and combustion. This made the 'Shooter's combustion more efficient than its rivals over a broader range of revs, also permitting the safe use of higher compression ratios. Even in roadster form, the "21" generated only 20 per cent less power than an F-head twin with almost three times the displacement.

The Peashooter's other "ace" was Joe Petrali who (along with Scott Parker) is surely the most successful racer ever to grace the race tracks of America. In 1935, towards the end of the model's racing career, he won every one of the 13 dirt track races in the national series. The diminutive Californian was equally adept whether board racing or tackling towering hill-climbs, proving virtually unbeatable until his retirement in 1938.

Petrali and the single first hit the headlines when the AMA adopted a new 21-inch racing class in 1925. In the first race under the new formula, fittingly held in Milwaukee before a crowd of over 20,000, Petrali, Jim Davis and Eddie Brock simply blasted the opposition into the Wisconsin weeds. Board-racing versions of the ohv roadster were stripped to the bare essentials, with tiny seats, "Speedster" drop handlebars and neither brakes nor mudguards. Such abbreviated devices were easily capable of speeds in excess of 80mph (128kph). Depending on the

type of competition, they were built with single-speed (Model SM) or three-speed (SA) transmission.

Despite the ohv single's instant track success, Juneau Avenue was oddly disposed towards its side-valve sidekick since the flathead roadster was seen as the likeliest seller. However, others quickly saw the potential of high-revving overhead-valve engines, and the Peashooter became the single of choice on the American racing scene (although a speedway version, inspired by the all-conquering British JAP, was far less successful).

The final, flattering piece in the Peashooter jigsaw came with the introduction of the ohv Knucklehead in 1936.

Although the factory was developing overhead-valve DAH competition twins during the late 1920s, the Knuckle bears many detail similarities with the Peashooter top end.

Whether this was by design or accident, no-one can now tell.

■ LEFT
*"Speedster" drop
handlebars were
a feature of
the Peashooter.*

WR/WRTT, 1940–51

Harley-Davidson's racing mainstay of the 1940s, the side-valve WR, had the humblest of beginnings, evolving by degrees from the unpretentious Model D of 1929. Essentially, this was powered by little more than a pair of Ricardo heads grafted from the 21.1cu in (346cc) single (which had almost the same bore diameter) onto a common crankcase. The machine developed rapidly year-on-year, becoming the Model R in 1932, at which time its hottest roadster derivative was the RLD Special Sport Solo.

Racing efforts at the time, both official and private, were concentrated on overhead valve engines, both singles and 45-inch twins. However, by 1933 the RLDE twin with magnesium alloy pistons was available from the factory by special order.

Two years later still, the Series R range included five models based on the familiar flathead "45", crowned by the lean and purposeful RLDR Competition Special – a snip at $322. For 1937, a

■ ABOVE *This "45" wears telescopic forks manufactured long after the side-valve racer was history.*

Knucklehead-inspired restyle and a welter of engine improvements metamorphosed the R into the enduring Model W. Other than the change of prefix letter, the 45-inch range continued as before, now with the WLDR Competition Special at its head – a WR in all but name. Harley-Davidson put this right in 1941: the WLDR still existed, but now as a mere Special Sport Solo roadster.

Taking its place as the hottest 45 was the plain WR, a race machine available only to special order. Initially, availability was poor – just 36 WRs were produced in 1941 – but both

SPECIFICATIONS	
Engine	side valve 4-stroke V-twin
Capacity	45.3cu in (742cc)
Transmission	3- or 4-speed
Power	40bhp
Wheelbase	60in (1,525mm)
Top speed	around 105mph (169kph)

■ ABOVE AND LEFT *Although substantially similar engines propelled American postmen, the WR carried Harley's racing banner for a decade in both factory and private teams.*

■ RIGHT *The main advantage of the side-valve twin wasn't its potency, but its capacity, which kept it competitive in American racing.*

■ LEFT *A competitor fettles his "45" during a modern classic race meeting.*

■ BELOW *The "pillion" pad helped the rider stretch out to cheat the wind.*

45 inches was unimpressive. Yet this, and sheer weight of numbers, was enough to rival the much more sophisticated but sorely handicapped overhead-valve twins and overhead-camshaft singles from Europe. The brute toughness of the WRTT, in particular, made it a surprisingly capable "Class C" racer. This formula had first been introduced for roadster-based machines in the 1920s to reduce the spiralling cost of Class A and B factory specials.

For more than a decade, these outwardly primitive machines gave a good account of themselves on the race tracks of America – taking 19 out of 23 championship victories in 1948 alone.

This was partly because they were rugged and dependable, and partly because the AMA was as eager then as it has been since to adjust the rules in favour of domestic hardware.

In this case the AMA, which is the governing body of American motorcycle sport, greeted the arrival of fast European overhead-valve machines with a decree that said they would be limited to 500cc, while side-valves of 750cc were permitted. And guess who made the only flathead racers in the frame?

demand and supply picked up dramatically in the aftermath of war. A total of 292 were produced in 1948, 121 in 1949 and 23 in the last year of production.

These purpose-built racing machines were, of course, very much stripped down compared to their roadster cousins (the WR had not so much as a front mudguard, and later examples also benefited from a lightweight chrome-molybdenum steel chassis). The WRTT, produced as a specific model only late in the WR's career, retained the heavier roadster frame. Being a flat-track machine, the WR also had no brakes, while the road-racing TT machine was equipped with standard WL wheels and brakes – scarcely state-of-the-art stopping power. The WR's suspension was no more impressive, with old-fashioned girder front forks and a rigid rear end. For good measure, the gearbox, although available with close-ratio racing cogs, was hand-change. It may have been crude, and 40bhp from

KR/KRTT
1952–69

What Harley-Davidson needed to replace the elderly WR was a machine reflecting the technology of its era. In the KR, the company most certainly didn't get it. What it got instead was yet another long-stroke flathead racer derived from a road bike, in this case the 45.3cu in (742cc) Model K which was about to be so comprehensively licked by British machines on America's streets. In racing, the KR had an edge: the AMA's 500cc limit on overhead-valve engines still applied.

As with the WR a decade earlier, production began slowly, with just 17 KRs built in the first year. Yet by 1955, the special equipment range encompassed no less than five specific models: the KHK Super Sport Solo, KHRM off-roader, KR dirt track racer, and KRTT and KHRTT "Tourist Trophy" machines.

All three KH models boasted the new 55cu in (883cc) long-stroke K-Series engine and were essentially "race replicas" intended as much for the

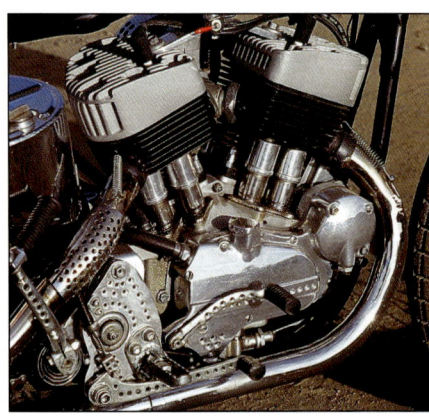

private enthusiast as the racer. Serious racers remained limited to what the regulations allowed: 750cc.

In 1955, the factory built 90 45-inch competition models, declining to 33 by the decade's end. Unlike the

WR/WRTT, all variants now enjoyed a lightweight racing frame, although only the road-racing TT model received the new swinging-arm rear end.

The flat-track KR had a smaller tank, fatter wheels and tyres and no need of brakes. Bore and stroke were identical to the WR's at 70 x 97mm (the slow-revving 55's stroke was even longer at 116mm).

However, the cylinders were commonly re-bored after bedding-in. By using the maximum permitted piston oversize – more than 0.04in (1.1mm) mechanics could raise the displacement legally to 46.8cu in (767cc).

At 9:1, the compression ratio was high by side-valve standards and a single 33mm Linkert carburettor was

SPECIFICATIONS	
Engine	side-valve 4-stroke V-twin
Capacity	45.3 cu in (742cc)
Transmission	4-speed
Power	48bhp
Weight	377–385lbs (171–175g)
Wheelbase	56in (1,420mm)
Top speed	150mph (240kph) (with road-race streamlining)

■ RIGHT *Rear springing identifies this KR as the TT version.*

standard. Power was around 48bhp at 7,000rpm, with 50lb/ft (68Nm) of torque at 5,000rpm. British Norton, Matchless and Triumph machines, as well as putting out far more specific power than the KR, handled and stopped far better. Yet the old KRs just kept rolling on.

While they were heavy (around 380lbs/172kg) and ill-suited to any circuit with proper corners, they remained surprisingly competitive elsewhere – not least because every race grid in America seemed to be packed with them.

Since a dirt-track KR actually cost $95 less than a stock road-going

Sportster during the mid-1960s, perhaps this wasn't too surprising.

The road racers, too, were capable of surprising feats. At the super-fast Daytona Speedway, streamlined KRs have been recorded in excess of 150mph (240kph), an astonishing achievement for a side-valve machine.

For all their shortcomings, in the hands of racing aces such as Markel and Resweber, they managed to win a round dozen American national titles during their 18 years on the grid.

The KR's astonishing span came to an end in 1969 when the AMA ended discriminatory limitations on overseas machines.

Faced with a level playing field, there was no way that the redoubtable old flathead "45" could compete with the machines that were coming in from abroad.

■ ABOVE RIGHT *A KRTT in Harley's famous orange and black factory racing colours.*

■ RIGHT *This dirt tracker wears TT-type rear suspension and brakes, although both the shock absorbers and front forks are non-period items.*

XR750 FLAT-TRACKER, 1970–PRESENT

To many people's eyes – and ears – the XR750 dirt-track machine is the most handsome, the raunchiest and the most purposeful piece of kit ever to rumble out of Milwaukee. Certainly no other Harley-Davidson has enjoyed so much competition success over so many years as the seminal XR. After almost two decades plugging along on the side-valve KR twin, the arrival of an overhead-valve replacement in 1970 must have been keenly anticipated. Yet its debut year was to prove a deep disappointment when Mert Lawwill and Mark Brelsford could manage only a disappointing sixth and seventh in the AMA championship. Just 12 months earlier, Lawwill had won the title on a side-valve KR.

The problem was the new engine's iron cylinders. They were heavy and conducted heat much less efficiently than aluminium components. This in

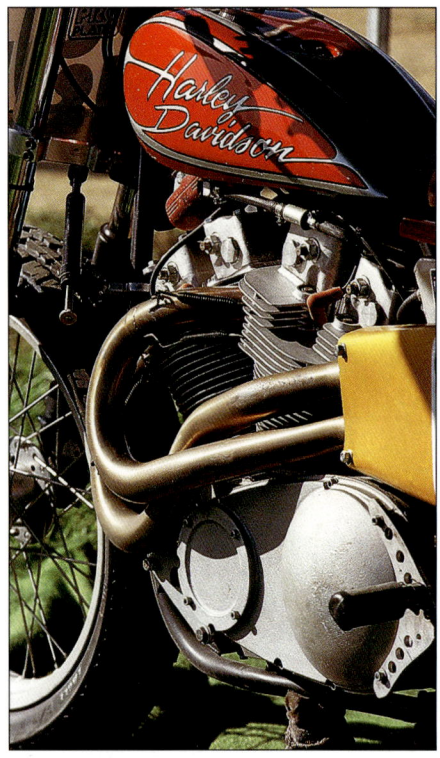

SPECIFICATIONS	
Engine	ohv V-twin
Capacity	45.8cu in (750cc)
Transmission	4-speed
Power	around 95 bhp
Weight	290lbs (132kg)
Top speed	130mph (210kph)

turn meant that the motor's compression ratio had to be drastically reduced – to around 8:1 – if fatal breakdowns were to be avoided. With lumpier pistons, the iron XR had proven fast – but it just couldn't last the distance. In 1970, race boss Dick O'Brien admitted to a lowly 62bhp at 6,200rpm. In June 1971, light alloy replaced iron, and the XR750 hasn't looked back.

■ **ABOVE LEFT** *Despite troubled beginnings, the XR went on to sweep away all before it in American dirt-track racing – with only occasional help from the rules when Honda's RS750 got too close.*

■ **LEFT** *Only that ugly California-mandated silencer mars the XR750's brutal yet beautiful lines.*

■ LEFT *The XR was also briefly successful in road racing, notably with Cal Rayborn in control. This is the iron-head machine on which he won the 1972 Transatlantic Series.*

On dirt, Mark Brelsford took the XR to the 1972 American Number One plate in its maiden season. At Easter the same year, the great Cal Rayborn whipped all comers in the annual USA v Great Britain road-race series.

At the heart of the XR is that rarest of beasts, a short-stroke Harley-Davidson. "Iron-head" XRs used what were essentially de-stroked 883cc Sportster engines, retaining the road machine's 72mm bore but with a shorter 82mm stroke. The 1972 engine's cylinders measured 79.4 x 75.8mm – by comparison, the side-valve KR measured an ultra-long-stroke 70 x 97mm. This, allied to a much stronger crankshaft, permitted more revs as well as a substantially higher 10.5:1 compression ratio made possible by the use of light alloy. The result was a dramatic rise in power and reliability. Shortly after Rayborn's Transatlantic road-race triumph (which was, ironically, on an iron-head engine), peak power was reputed to be around 80bhp at 8,000rpm. Even so, for many years even the light alloy XR ran dangerously hot – road-racers employed two oil coolers yet were worn out after only 200 miles (320km) – until the internal oil circulation was improved.

At the outset, carburation was by twin 1½in (36mm) Japanese Mikuni instruments (often larger on the road racers). Sparks were provided by a Fairbanks-Morse magneto, an unreliable system sometimes dubbed "Can't Get

■ ABOVE *They still fight for it: the coveted AMA Number One plate.*

■ BELOW *Nine times AMA Number One Scott Parker, here in action at Sacramento. All his titles have been XR-powered.*

Worse" by unhappy riders. The lightweight, high-grade steel frame used Ceriani forks and paired Girling rear shock absorbers. Dry weight was a feather-light 291lb (132kg), although the road racers, with a fairing and brakes, were somewhat heavier.

Almost 30 years of detailed development have left the XR engine little changed visually, but without equal for the demands of dirt-track competition.

These days, power is around 95bhp at 7,800rpm, with a strong spread from 4,500 to more than 8,000rpm. On one mile (1.61km) ovals, this is good for a top speed of around 130mph (210kph), although it's the way that the big twin finds grip that really sets it apart from the others on the field.

True, the XR soon became obsolete as a road racer, but has gone from strength to strength on the dirt tracks of the United States.

In the hands of men like Brelsford, Gary Scott, Jay Springsteen and Scott Parker, the XR has simply swept away all before it, taking three-quarters of all the subsequent AMA championships.

RR250, RR350 1971–6

The twin cylinder, two-stroke racers built at Varese during the 1970s brought Harley-Davidson its sole successes in post-war grand prix road racing. These were state-of-the-art machines, broadly similar to the stroker twins produced by Yamaha and Kawasaki, with fierce powerbands, strident exhaust notes and performance belying their relatively small engine displacement. To cope with the narrow band of usable revs, the gearbox held six speeds – and might well have held more if this were not prohibited by FIM regulations.

The 250's 56.2 x 50mm cylinders were fed via rotary disc valves by twin 34mm Mikuni carburettors. The earliest examples were air-cooled but the factory soon switched to liquid-cooling, bringing far greater temperature stability and reliability during long grand prix races. Primary drive was by gear, to a multi-plate dry clutch and thence to the six-speed "box". Power output was prodigious (particularly by Milwaukee's four-stroke standards), with the 250 producing 58bhp at 12,000rpm and the 350 a dozen horsepower more at 11,400rpm. The 250's figure equates to over 232bhp per litre, compared to a mere 65 for the KR750 which had been Harley-Davidson's racing mainstay at the time RR250 development began.

■ LEFT *The great Walter Villa at speed on the RR250 at the notorious Nurburgring circuit in 1978. He failed to finish. Note that the machine still relies on a drum front brake.*

SPECIFICATIONS: RR250	
Engine	liquid-cooled twin cylinder 2-stroke
Capacity	15.1cu in (248cc)
Transmission	6-speed
Peak power	58bhp @12,000rpm
Weight	230lbs (104kg)
Top speed	140mph (225kph)

■ BELOW LEFT *A disc-braked factory two-stroke twin shares pride of place with a classic four-stroke single.*

■ BELOW RIGHT *Villa on the RR350 at Hockenheim in 1977, carrying the world champion's Number One. He finished third in the 250cc world championship that year, but the 350 proved less competitive.*

The chassis featured a conventional twin cradle of high-grade tubular steel. Italian Ceriani suspension graced the front end with a pair of English Girling shock absorbers at the rear. The whole package weighed just 230lbs (104kg). If the machine had a shortcoming, it was the use of drum brakes (albeit a double-sided twin-leading shoe affair at the front) when hydraulic discs were already in widespread use and far superior. Discs finally arrived in 1976, by which time the great Walter Villa had already taken two 250cc world titles.

With better brakes, he repeated the feat in 1976, adding the 350cc title for good measure. RRs also campaigned successfully in American road races, ridden by Gary Scott, Jay Springsteen, Cal Rayborn and others.

MX250 1977-8

Harley-Davidson's only venture into mainstream motocross produced a highly competitive machine which could have become better still had Milwaukee not severed its Italian links after just two years of MX production. By the time the MX250 came on stream in 1977, Varese had developed a formidable pool of two-stroke know-how, not least from its successful grand prix road-racing experience.

Four years after its official demise, the great Jay Springsteen mischievously used an MX-based machine to win the first AMA event of the 1982 season in Houston. We can only speculate about where this potential might have led.

The single-cylinder stroker used a short-stroke (72 x 59.6mm) engine which drove an integral five-speed transmission via gear primary drive and wet multi-plate clutch – such as you might find on any dirt-bike today.

Initial examples were air-cooled, but a liquid-cooled version came later. A 38mm Italian dell'Orto carburettor provided the fuel (mixed 20:1 with oil for lubrication), while sparks came from a CDI generator on the left end of the crankshaft. During development, peak power rose to a ferocious 58bhp

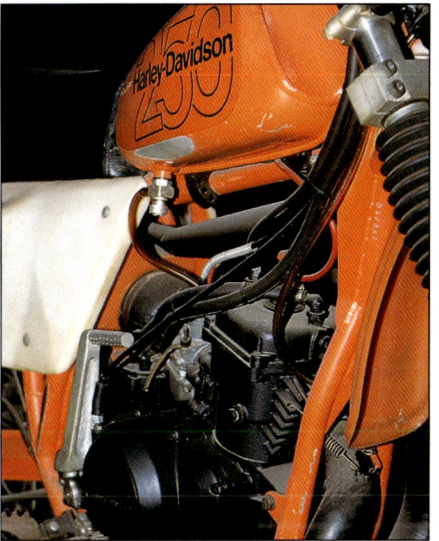

■ ABOVE AND LEFT *Harley's Italian-designed and built MX250 motocrosser benefited from lessons learned in grand prix road racing and might have gone on to great things had Varese not been sold.*

at a giddy 12,000rpm. Telescopic forks provided a generous 9in (228mm) of travel with a similar degree of movement that came from the twin rear shock absorbers.

Light alloy Akront rims were laced to simple 5½in (140mm) drum brakes (as discs were not yet used on dirt-bikes).

SPECIFICATIONS	
Engine	single-cylinder 2-stroke
Capacity	14.8cu in (242cc)
Transmission	5-speed
Peak power	58bhp @12,000rpm
Weight	233lbs (106kg)
Wheelbase	57.3in (1,455mm)
Top speed	n/a

■ RIGHT *Harley's only current single is this Rotax-engined device.*

AERMACCHI OHV RACERS 1961–78

Originally an aircraft factory – hence the name – Aermacchi diversified into motorcycle production in 1948, in Varese, Italy. Its first models were 123cc (7.5cu in) singles – two-strokes but already possessing the horizontal cylinder which was to become so typical of the marque. Overhead valve four-stroke singles followed, both road bikes and the potent Ala D'Oro (Golden Wing) production racer. A generation of elegant racing models were developed from the late 1950s onwards, based on this Alfredo Bianchi-designed machine.

Although the racers were built in both 250cc (15cu in) and 350cc (21cu in) versions, it was the latter which achieved the greater success. Even during the 1960s, a single-cylinder push-rod machine was an anachronism among the exotica then crowding the grands prix grids, yet the "Macchi" exploited its fine handling, light weight and slim aerodynamic profile to the fullest. Its best world-championship performance came in 1966 when the late Renzo Pasolini – the "Paso" in

■ LEFT *An Aermacchi 250 at speed. Light weight and a slim profile made them astonishingly fast.*

■ BELOW LEFT *A CRTT 250 in factory racing livery.*

SPECIFICATIONS: 350	
Engine	ohv horizontal single
Capacity	344cc (21cu in)
Transmission	5-speed
Power	38bhp
Weight	245lbs (111kg)
Wheelbase	not known
Top Speed	130mph (210kph)

the Ducati model of the same name – took third place in the 350cc grand prix championship.

It was as a privateer mount that the little "Macchi" achieved its greatest popularity and success however, although it also had a reputation for being temperamental unless expertly set up. Perhaps its most remarkable performance came in the 1970 Isle of Man TT races when Alan Barnett lapped the daunting Mountain Course at a stunning 99.32mph (159.84kph) on a Syd Lawton 350, recording well over 40mpg (15km/litre) in the process.

Nor were the ohv single's exploits confined to the track. On 21 October 1965, a 250cc Aermacchi established a world mile record of 176.817mph (284.55kph) and kilometre record of 285.21kph (177.225mph) at Utah's Bonneville salt flats. Although nominally a Sprint roadster, the machine in question used a 1966-specification CR racing engine on standard pump fuel. Officially, Milwaukee dubbed its Italian singles CR, CRS and CRTT, although in Europe these designations were largely ignored.

The single was produced with many variations over the years, but the 350's

■ BELOW *A brace of ex-factory racers. Note the racing dry clutch.*

■ BELOW *A 350 'Macchi contesting the 1984 Historic Isle of Man TT. Ironically this was the only TT ever won by an American – on a British Matchless machine.*

typical power output was around 38bhp at 8,400rpm. Bore and stroke were under-square at 74 x 80mm, although this incurred a dangerously high piston speed (almost 4,400ft/1,340m) at maximum revs. As a result, other configurations were also built, including short stroke and ultra-short stroke examples. Compression was high – around 11.4:1 – and the engine breathed through a 35mm dell'Orto carburettor tipped almost vertically to feed fuel into the horizontal cylinder. A short megaphone exhaust swept down the right side of the machine.

The racer was available with a choice of "A" or "B" gear clusters, the latter offering the closer ratios, although the engine delivered a reasonable spread of power considering its high state of tune.

The chassis was simple in the extreme, using a large-diameter tubular steel spine, which was reputed to flex but in a controlled, user-friendly way which gave the rider ample feedback.

A variety of suspension and brake components were employed, invariably with telescopic forks (usually Ceriani), twin rear shock absorbers and drum

brakes. On later versions, the front drum was often twin-sided.

A measure of the machine's excellence is the sheer joy – and speed – with which many contest classic races today.

■ LEFT *Pictured here, the engine of a 1969 350 Aermacchi.*

■ BELOW *In the USA, Aermacchis derived from the Sport roadster were also popular for dirt-track racing.*

LUCIFER'S HAMMER, 1983

■ BELOW *Lucifer's Hammer's engine was based on that of an XR750 competition model.*

In the spring of 1983, Lucifer's Hammer was the first big twin for a decade to carry Harley-Davidson's famous black and orange racing livery on to the Daytona speed bowl. It certainly did so with distinction, taking the great Jay Springsteen – better known as a dirt-track rider but certainly no slouch on tarmac – to victory in the Battle of the Twins event. In October of the same year, Gene Church began a love affair with the same machine when he rode it triumphantly in the BoT finals, also held at Daytona.

The Hammer represented one of those bouts of enthusiasm and expertise with the big twin that were often typical of Harley-Davidson. The germ of the project began when Dave McClure rode a prototype XR1000 street bike at Daytona the previous autumn, which

SPECIFICATIONS	
Engine	ohv V-twin
Capacity	60.9cu in (998cc)
Transmission	4-speed
Power	104bhp
Weight	286lbs (130kg)
Wheelbase	56in (1,420mm)
Top speed	158mph (254kph)

suggested that a full-on racer project might succeed. Once race-boss Dick O'Brien got the go-ahead to build what would become the Springsteen machine, he set his hand-picked team into action. Engine work was put in the hands of Don Habermehl, while racing legend Carroll Resweber (four times AMA

champion for Harley, 1958 to 1961) put his considerable talents into the chassis, and Peter Zylstra oversaw the design. To some extent, the machine was also a test-bed and publicity statement for the XR1000 roadster unveiled at the same Daytona meeting, another project which very much carried the O'Brien imprint.

The engine consisted of a modified competition XR750 bottom end and light alloy heads mated to iron Sportster barrels. Twin 42mm smoothbore Mikuni carburettors took care of induction, feeding exotic 110 octane aviation fuel – for nothing less would handle the engine's giddy 10.5:1 compression ratio. To improve combustion, each cylinder boasted twin spark plugs, fired by a total-loss racing ignition system.

In dyno tests, this device had put out a brutal 106bhp at 7,500rpm, but fears comprehensively crashed by then-AMA champion Mark Brelsford at Daytona fully ten years before the Hammer's 1983 win. The basic single spine and twin tube cradle was heavily reworked with extra gussets and bracing, mated to an all-new box-section swing-arm.

The rest was essentially an Italian affair: front suspension was in the hands of a pair of 1.57in (40mm) Forcelli Italia forks, with twin Fox gas shock absorbers at the rear. Brembo supplied the brakes: twin 11.8in (300mm) floating-front disc brakes, with a 9.8in (250mm) disc at the rear. These ran on Campagnolo magnesium wheels, 16in (406mm) front wheel, 18in (457mm) rear, both shod with Goodyear racing slick tyres. Dry weight was a remarkably lean 285lbs (130kg) and top speed an even more impressive 158mph (254kph).

After its winning Daytona debut, Gene Church went on to take the HOG-sponsored Hammer to three AMA Battle of the Twins titles.

All of this success was not really too bad for a bike that began its life as a ten-year-old scrap!

about reliability caused Habermehl to impose a rev ceiling of 7,000rpm, at which point the big twin was pumping out 104bhp. Since even this equated to a dizzying mean piston speed of 4,430 ft/min (1,350m/min), the precaution must have been wise. Not only was power prodigious but the spread was enormous, too, coming in strongly by 4,000rpm. A four-speed gearbox was more than adequate. Resweber's chassis employed the very XR750 frame

VR1000, 1994– PRESENT

The VR1000, which has been flying Milwaukee's road-racing flag through the latter half of the 1990s is a Harley even the faithful scarcely believe. It's a V-twin, true, but with twin overhead camshafts, and its cylinders are liquid-cooled and splayed at a sacrilegious 60 degrees. True, its four valves per cylinder have been done by Milwaukee before – but not for 70-odd years.

Clearly the VR is not your typical Hog. It's built in the United States, says "Harley-Davidson" on the side, and is decked out in classic black and orange racing livery. But it probably doesn't share a single part with any other Milwaukee model.

The machine uses Harley's own purpose-built powerplant, which looks for all the world like one quarter of a V8 car engine in its design and construction. Almost everything else is bought-in from quality suppliers, such as Swedish Ohlins

■ ABOVE *Chris Carr in action on the VR1000 at Daytona Raceway. In 1999, Carr returned to dirt track and claimed the AMA title.*

SPECIFICATIONS

Engine	dohc V-twin
Capacity	60.8cu in (996cc)
Transmission	6-speed
Power	171bhp
Weight	373lbs (169kg)
Wheelbase	55.1in (1,400mm)
Top speed	179mph (288kph)

suspension and Italian Marchesini magnesium-alloy cast wheels. The whole is tied together, not by American steel, but by a massively stiff twin-beam aluminium chassis. Erik Buell was one of the original development engineers on the project, while the race team is run by Steve Shybee.

In its early years, ridden by the mercurial Miguel du Hamel, the VR proved surprisingly potent, pumping out more than 120bhp at 10,800rpm. Yet it did not make the progress for which Harley fans might have hoped. This was not for the want of talented riders. Among others, the twin has been ridden

■ ABOVE *As brutally black as the old XLCR, the factory racer has failed to live up to expectations on the track.*

by AMA Number 1 Chris Carr, Thomas Wilson, Doug Chandler and former World Superbike champion Scott Russell. The bike continued to improve, but not quickly enough. Observers were often surprised at the lack of all-out effort the factory appeared to put into the project. As a racer, it had one fatal and embarrassing flaw: it didn't win. No wonder onlookers – Harley devotees and not – struggled to comprehend quite what the VR1000 was for.

Even the VR's noted tractability could not overcome this sort of deficit. Although it could be competitive in wet conditions, it lacked at least 30bhp compared to similar Ducati twins. During 1998–9, however, an intensive programme of development work began to show startling results. Peak power soared to more than 170bhp, giving a measured top speed of 179mph (288kph) around the Daytona banking. Rider Pascal Picotte, in particular,

posted some impressive results during 1999, although he could manage no better than twelfth place in the American MBNA Superbike championship. Team mate Scott Russell placed twentieth.

Some VRs have been sold to private teams, with an odd route to racing legality. To qualify for competition, these must be street-legal – not necessarily in the USA, but somewhere. The United States is a very expensive place to make any motorcycle legal, so a limited-edition run of 50 "roadster" VRs flew a flag of convenience. No, not Liberia, but the truth is almost as absurd. The VR1000 met the relevant standards for road-going motorcycles – in Poland.

Nonetheless, this high-tech device – the only racer in the world, for instance, to run a carbon multi-plate clutch – remains a puzzle. What is the purpose of the VR1000? Is it a rolling test-bed for hardware that might appear on future roadsters? Or is it the basis for a future roadster model? Racing people close to the factory team have suggested that a road-going liquid-cooled sports bike may be a genuine possibility. Some even believe that such a device could blow away even a Ducati V-twin; traditional Harley die-hards must throw up their hands in horror at the very thought. Wherever you stand, like the rest of us, you'll just have to wait and see.

Air cleaner: A filter for removing dust from the air entering the engine.

Air-cooled: An engine which is cooled directly by the air flowing over it, rather than via a liquid-filled radiator.

Alternator: An electrical generator producing alternating current which must then be converted to direct current by a rectifier.

AMA: American Motorcycle Association (governing body of American bike racing).

Bearing: Placed between two rubbing or turning components to reduce friction. Can be "plain" or with moving balls or rollers.

bhp (brake horsepower): Engine power as measured on a dynamometer, on which the engine is run against a resistance or "brake". Horsepower is essentially torque times revs.

Big end: The connection between con-rod and crankshaft.

Bore: Diameter of the cylinder in which the piston travels.

Bottom end: The engine below the cylinder, containing crankshaft, bearings, oil pump, etc.

CAD: Computer-aided design.

Camshaft: A lobed shaft turning at half engine speed which operates the valves.

Carburettor: Instrument that mixes fuel and air for combustion.

Choke: A device that enriches the fuel and air mixture to facilitate cold starts; also the carburettor venturi.

Clutch: A device which allows the rear wheel to be isolated from the turning of the engine.

Coil: An electrical device which turns low-voltage current into high-voltage for the spark plug.

Compression: The extent to which the piston "squeezes" the fuel and air mixture, expressed as a ratio of maximum to minimum volume.

Con-rod (connecting rod): A (usually steel) member connecting the crankshaft to the piston.

Crankcases: The (usually aluminium) housing containing bottom end components. These are commonly split into pairs.

Crankshaft: An eccentric (cranked) shaft on which the con-rods run, held in the crankcases by the main bearings; it turns the piston's reciprocating action into rotary motion.

Cylinder: A cylindrical "barrel" in which the piston moves up and down.

Disc: A type of brake in which "pads" of friction material are squeezed against rotating disc(s) attached to the wheel.

Displacement: An engine's capacity, i.e. total volume displaced by an engine's pistons.

Drum: A type of brake in which a mechanism forces "shoes" against the inside of a drum in the wheel hub.

Dry-sump: An engine in which lubricating oil is located in a separate tank rather than the sump.

Evo: The 1,340cc V2 Evolution engine produced from 1984.

F-head: An ioe cylinder head.

Flathead: Any side-valve engine.

Flywheel: A heavy disc spinning with the crankshaft which stores engine inertia and "smooths out" power pulses.

Gearbox: A housing in which lie the shafts on which the transmission gears run.

Gudgeon pin (wrist pin in the USA): A steel tube connecting the piston to the small end.

Hardtail: A rigid, i.e. unsprung, motorcycle rear end.

Hog: Nickname given to any Harley-Davidson model.

HOG: Harley Owners' Group.

Horsepower: Torque times revs, the actual power output of an engine. However, in the early years, an engine's rated horsepower was simply a function of engine displacement.

Hydraulic: Operated by pressure in a fluid, as with disc brakes or hydraulic "lifters".

ioe (inlet-over-exhaust): The earliest type of valve arrangement, with a side exhaust valve facing an overhead inlet valve. The latter could be "automatic" or mechanically operated.

Knucklehead: Harley's first ohv engine, 1936–47.

Lifter (USA): A push-rod. Also hydraulic lifters.

Magneto: An early, free-standing device which generates (and times) the ignition spark.

Mudguard: fender (USA).

ohv (overhead valve): Both valves contained in the cylinder head and actuated by rockers.

Panhead: An ohv Harley engine produced 1948–65.

Piston: An inverted cylindrical "tub" in the cylinder which transmits combustion forces to the crankshaft via the con-rod.

Piston ring: A flexible iron or steel ring located in a groove near the top of the piston which seals against the leakage of combustion gases or oil.

Power: See bhp.

Push-rod (also, solid lifter in the USA): A metal rod which transmits camshaft motion to the valve via the rocker.

Rake: The effective angle of the front forks, expressed in degrees from vertical.

Revs (rpm): Engine revolutions per minute.

Retro-Tech: Modern technology that mimicks old, such as Springer forks.

Rocker: A rocking arm which transmits motion from lifter to the valve.

Shovelhead: An ohv Harley engine produced 1966–84.

Side-valve: "Flathead" engines with both valves below the level of the cylinder head.

Small end (little end): The connection between the piston's gudgeon pin and the con-rod.

Softail: Rear suspension with swing arm and underslung shock absorbers, that is designed to look like a hardtail.

Springer: A modern "Retro-Tech" version of the sprung fork; any Harley-Davidson so fitted.

Sprung fork: Pre-1948 front suspension with solid legs, and (usually) coil spring(s) at the top.

Stroke: The distance travelled by a piston between its top-most and bottom-most points.

Swing-arm: Also known as swinging fork, a pivoting suspension member allowing the rear wheel to move up and down.

Sump: An extension at the bottom of the crankcase containing oil. "Dry sump" engines hold their oil in a separate tank.

Tachometer (rev-counter): An instrument that measures engine revs.

Telescopic fork: Front suspension in which one tube (containing a spring) slides within another, damped by oil.

Timing: Arranging that the spark is delivered (or the valves open and close) at the correct time.

Top end: The engine "above" the base of the cylinder, including the cylinder head.

Trail (castor): The extent to which the front tyre's contact patch trails the point at which the steering angle intersects the ground. Harley-Davidson favours high trail figures which tend to give slower steering and greater stability.

Torque: The turning force applied to the crankshaft (and ultimately the rear wheel) by the force of combustion on the piston.

Venturi: The part of the carburettor through which incoming air passes; also its diameter.

Wheelbase: Distance between the front and rear wheel centres.

Wrist Pin: see gudgeon pin.

The Harley-Davidson company has always favoured a particularly cryptic method of model designation, although the system is in most cases quite simple once the "code" is understood. The first model made in any numbers was the 1908 Model 4 – indicating the fourth year of production. A suffix letter identified the precise model type, such as "A" for magneto ignition, with the most basic model simply known by its model year number. The first "suffix" was actually a prefix: in 1912, "X" before the model year indicated a rear wheel clutch.

Thus, the Model 5 followed in 1909, the Model 6 in 1910 and so on, until all models adopted the last two digits of their year of manufacture from 1916 (Models 16). Thus, Model 16B was a base-model 1916 single, a 16E was the most basic twin and a 16J was a three-speed twin with full electrical system. Unfortunately, Harley's long-standing habit of having lead times – by which you could buy most "year 2000" models in late 1999, for instance, often creates additional ambiguity.

Later, as the range became entirely composed of V-twins, the suffix letters became more elaborate and numerous but the basic year-prefix system continued publicly until 1969 (and technically still does). Initially, there was little attempt to marry a suffix letter logically with what it represented, although in recent times the connection has – usually – been more clear.

Not quite every letter of the alphabet has been used ("Y" is the exception) which would be daunting enough, but several have enjoyed different meanings at different times. Equally, the same

"feature" has also commanded different code letters. Thus, electric start has been indicated variously by "B" and "E", while the latter has also represented the 61-inch Knucklehead and Panhead engines (as opposed to "F" for the 74-inch models) and even police spec. In recent times, "B" has variously represented Belt drive, Daytona and Bad Boy, to name but three.

All current Harley-Davidsons start with a pair of letters, denoting certain engine and chassis combinations. Therefore, XL is the Sportster range, with solidly-mounted 883cc or 1,200cc engines. The suffix dates back to the original 55-inch XL Sportster of 1957.

"FX" first appeared for the 1971 SuperGlide when the "X" indicated that the model had borrowed the lighter Sportster front end. The FX suffix now refers to a welter of models with Twin Cam or 81.6cu in (1,340cc) Evo engines. FXD now represents the Dyna series with two-point rubber-mounted engines dating from the FXDB Sturgis frame of 1991. FXST denotes Softails, with engines rigidly mounted in a chassis based on the previous FX range.

"Heavyweight" models (not that most others are light) have enjoyed the FL suffix since 1941, when "F" indicated the new 74-inch Knucklehead engine, of which the Special Sport version was designated "L". These days, it refers to rubber-mounted big twin engines: Electra and TourGlides. Exceptions to this are rigidly-mounted FLST Softail models, such as the Fat Boy and Heritage Softail.

The table on the right outlines a selection of the suffix letters that have been employed.

Suffix	Modern meaning	Historical meaning
A	–	Army (military spec)/without tow bar (on Servi-Car)
B	Bad, as in Bad Boy, Belt Drive and Daytona	Electric start/previously aluminium piston(s)
C	Custom, Classic, Café (as in Café Racer)	"Competition"/Commercial /Canadian spec
CH	–	"Competition Hot": super sports with magneto
D	Dyna, Daytona	At least four other uses
DG	Disc Glide	–
E	(Formerly) electric start. Previously 61-inch ohv engine and some police models	–
F	Fat Boy	As a prefix, 74-inch ohv engine; as suffix, foot change
H	Notionally extra power but largely redundant	Extra power/high compression/larger engine
I	Fuel injection	–
J	–	Battery electrical system (as opposed to magneto)
L	–	Sports specification; "LD" signified Special Sports models
LR	Low Rider	–
N	Nostalgia	Iron piston
P	–	Police model/sprung fork on 1949 ohv models
Q	–	Two passenger sidecar
R	Road King	Racing/pseudo racing (XR1000)
S	Springer, as in the last letter of FXSTS (Springer Softail) or Sport, as in FLHS (ElectraGlide Sport)	Sidecar specifications/ sometimes Sport
SP	Sport Edition, as in FXRS-SP Low Rider Sport Edition	–
ST	Softail	–
T	Touring, with frame-mounting fairing	Reverse gear/Twin
U	Ultra	"Restricted" engines
WG	WideGlide	–
X	Some Sports models	Rear wheel clutch

PHOTOGRAPHY ACKNOWLEDGEMENTS:

The Publishers would like to thank the following for their kind permission to reproduce their photographs:

John Bolt
26–7, 29tl, 42b.

John Caroll
36br, 40t/mr/b, 41bl.

Alan Cathcart
122, 123t.

Bob Clarke
16, 39tr, 41m, 42t, 43b, 55b, 60–1, 81m, 103, 106–7, 112t, 113t/b, 115t/m, 117t, 118bl, 120b, 125.

Classic Bike
24b, 56b, 74b, 75t.

Neil Dalleywater
36bl, 64t, 105t.

Mac McDiarmid
2, 11tr, 14t, 22b, 23tr, 28t, 29tr/b, 33t, 44–5, 46, 48t, 49tl, 51t, 52m, 53t, 65t, 66t, 67tl, 68bl/br, 69tr, 78, 79t/m, 82–3, 84m/b, 85m, 86t/m, 87t/m, 90–1, 92t, 93t, 100–1, 116, 117m/b, 119m, 121tl/m, 123bl/br.

Don Morley
8–9, 17, 31, 118t/br, 119b, 120t, 121tr.

Quadrant
6, 54t, 99.

Tony Stone
35.

Garry Stuart
10, 11tl/b, 12, 13, 14b, 15, 18–19, 20, 21, 22t/m, 23tl/b, 24t, 25, 28m/b, 29m, 30, 32t/b, 33m/bl/br, 34t/b, 36t, 37, 38, 39tl, 39m/b, 40ml, 41bl, 42m, 43t, 47t/b, 48b, 49tr/b, 50, 51b, 52t, 54b, 55tl/tr, 58, 59, 62, 63, 64b, 65b, 66b, 67tr/b, 68t, 69tl/b, 70t, 71ml, 72–2, 75b, 76, 77, 79b, 80m/b, 81t, 85b, 86b, 94, 95, 96b, 108, 109, 110, 111, 112bl, 113m, 114m/b, 115b, 119t, 121, 124.

All other photographs courtesy of Harley-Davidson, Inc.

t=top b=bottom l=left r=right m=middle tr= top right tl=top left ml=middle left mr=middle right bl=bottom left br=bottom right lm=left middle tmr=top middle right tml=top middle left